FAYE BROWNLIE • SUSAN CLOSE

BEYOND CHALK & TALK

Collaborative strategies for the middle and high school years

Pembroke Publishers Limited

Dedication

To the adolescent within us all.

© 1992 Pembroke Publishers Limited
538 Hood Road
Markham, Ontario
L3R 3K9

Canadian Cataloguing in Publication Data

Brownlie, Faye
    Beyond chalk and talk: collaborative strategies
    for the middle and high school years

Includes bibliographical references.
ISBN 0-921217-49-8

1. Teaching.   2. Education, Secondary.
3. Education, Elementary.   I. Close, Susan.
II. Title.

LB1025.3.B76 1992   371.3'028'2   C92-094817-0

Editor: Joanne Close
Design: John Zehethofer
Cover Photography: Ajay Photographics
Typesetting: Jay Tee Graphics Ltd.

Printed and bound in Canada
9 8 7 6 5 4 3 2

Foreword

The class in which I was demonstrating had been discussing the issue of free trade and whether or not this was beneficial to the country. The discussion had been lively. We had examined the issue from several points of view. The source documents included several newspaper articles, an editorial, a magazine article, and personal reflections. Many questions had arisen from the small group and whole class interchange. Student voices had joined in skepticism, wonder, outrage, and passion. Seated among the students, the observing teachers waited for closure of the lesson.

''Can you take a few minutes to think back on this lesson? I would appreciate some input from you. If I were to conduct this lesson with another group of students, what advice would you give me to improve the learning opportunity for them?''

Stillness blanketed the room. Finally one student asked, ''You want us to tell you out loud?''

I nodded, another moment of quiet and astonishment, then the room erupted with voices again. The advice from these students ranged from ''Don't change our groups *so* often'' to Rob following me out of the class and down the hall. ''I have a few more things to tell you. . . . I was so actively involved in that lesson I will probably never forget it. . . . You never gave us any right answers. You kept pushing us to think, think, think, and to provide reasons for our opinions. This is what learning is all about! . . . Are you going to other classes to show other teachers these strategies? . . . Do you really know how much more we'd come to school if this way of working together and problem solving was common? This is the Year 2000, that new program!''

I wished I had a tape recorder to capture Rob's articulate burst of enthusiasm and support! Such testimony! Rob is a very articulate young man. He is also a spokesperson for our secondary students and his point is well made. We are at a point in our careers, as teachers, where we *do* know what to do to make a difference in learning so our students can put into practice the best of what we know. The challenge is to have this difference be more than an occasional event. Exceptional learning opportunities are possible for all students, in all classes, in all schools. It is time we moved beyond having a 'one best example' story to stories of 'this is the way it is' . . .

Acknowledgments

We are deeply indebted to those secondary teachers and administrators who welcomed us into their classrooms, their schools, their inquiry. Together we can make a difference in the lives of our students.

Karalee Close, our typist, has been our self-actualized learner. Thank you for your smiling patience and your skill.

The publishers gratefully acknowledge the following organizations and individuals for permission to reprint material in this book:

Excerpts from ''Whales dying in toxic St. Lawrence'' by Andre Picard. Reprinted with permission of *The Globe and Mail*.

H. Gardner in *Seven Ways of Knowing: Understanding Multiple Intelligence, Second Edition*, by D. Lazear. Copyright © 1991 by Skylight Publishing, Palatine, Illinois. Reprinted with permission of the publisher.

S. Jeroski and L. Kaser in *Reading and Responding: Evaluation Resources for Teachers* (Gr. 6) by S. Jeroski, F. Brownlie and L. Kaser. Copyright © 1991 by Nelson Canada, Scarborough, Ontario. Reprinted by permission of the publisher.

B. Marzano in *Tactics for Thinking* by Bob Marzano and D.E. Arrendondo. Copyright © 1986 by Mid-Continent Regional Educational Laboratory. Reprinted with permission by the author.

Every effort has been made to acknowledge all sources of material used in this book. The publisher would be grateful if any errors or omissions were pointed out, so that they may be corrected.

Contents

1

About the Book

Beyond Chalk and Talk: Collaborative strategies for the middle and high school years is our invitation to you to join us in a series of classrooms where we interact with our students. We invite you to collaborate with us in the examination of our practices and develop your personal 'wisdom of practice'. As a result of this case-study approach, you should be able to pull out the critical elements to personalize teaching and learning in whatever your current working context may be. Today's power shift, as we see it, happens when teachers and students grab hold of decision making and design learning sequences that work for them.

We work in classrooms as learners, with teachers. In our chapters, you will notice the voices of the teacher and of the students. You will also notice the observer or team of observers who participate in the lessons, and the sidebar of reflective thought—the framework we use to guide the moment-by-moment decisions that are made in the classroom.

Some of the students were already bent over their papers. Others searched the ceiling for possibilities, then responded. As we moved among them, I could see that many had asked questions, although most had thought that they would generate predictions. Several of the students had sketched.

Side Bar of Reflective Thought
Students are encouraged to change their strategy to fit the context.
Voice of the Observer(s)

TEACHER: Did anything surprise you about your response?

Voice of the Teacher

DAVE: I always predict. But those phrases were so weird I had to ask questions.

Voice of the Student

We begin this book by laying a foundation. We attempt to articulate:

- our belief system that frames the decisions we make,
- the attributes of a strategy,
- the 'big picture' or menu from which we choose our strategies,
- our focus on active learning, and
- our focus on the learner through Gardner's Multiple Intelligence Theory, or Seven Ways of Knowing.

Putting this foundation into practice, we have attempted to model a series of thinking/learning strategies in a variety of content areas in the secondary school. Beginning each chapter are several quotes that support the thinking behind the lesson design. Concluding each chapter is a synthesis of the strategy, a snapshot of the next day's lesson, and several cross-curricular examples. Examine these scenarios and adapt the lessons to increase the opportunities for success for all students in your classes.

Do not be afraid to read outside your content area! We have found that these strategies readily adapt to most areas and can be considered as ways of moving through content. Using a journey metaphor, it is the content that you choose that provides the territory of the map for the journey. Without the territory, learners have no place to go and without a focus on the learners, we have no information as to who is traveling, what baggage and skills they bring, and where they want to go. One tour package does not fit all! Without the strategies, learners are limited in their ways of traveling and may move from place to place without fully experiencing what is there to be enjoyed. They can return home unchanged, having toured but not traveled.

One is more likely to travel when engaged. This mandates that we put aside our chalk, stop talking, and begin to organize experiences for students that engage them with the content of the curriculum. The challenge is to stop telling and to start teaching! Without this shift, there is little chance that we will increase the numbers of students who become disciplinary experts within various fields of study.

Our content choices fuel student-to-student and teacher-to-student interactions, a change that is central to making learning happen. Effective teaching relies on wise decisions about content and process—decisions that involve the students and that match their learning needs. The decisions we make in our classes shift the power from outside the class to where it belongs—inside the class, where teachers and students are learning and teaching.

In 1986, at a conference on critical thinking, Debbie Walsh presented information on learner retention after a 24-hour period. The graphic representation she employed had a profound effect on our practice. It is an image that continually reminds us to step off the stage, to include the learners, and to organize for collaborative experiences. We have adapted Walsh's triangle to include more ways of knowing.

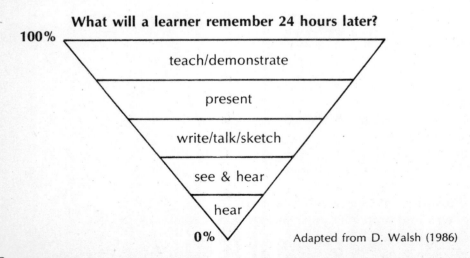

What will a learner remember 24 hours later?

100%
- teach/demonstrate
- present
- write/talk/sketch
- see & hear
- hear

0%

Adapted from D. Walsh (1986)

Walsh's research suggests that if we continue to lecture as the primary means of delivering content of the curriculum, most learners will retain only 10% of what we say. If we lecture with visuals, preferably color visuals, learners' retention levels will be increased. However, if we stop talking and invite learners to participate in making sense of the content by writing, talking, and sketching about it, that is, making meaning, they will remember even more! Retention is again increased if learners work with others and present what they know. But the most effective means of remembering is to teach and demonstrate an understanding, a reciprocal process involving negotiations of meaning. It is with this in mind that we choose strategies and design learning sequences.

An overview of the strategies discussed in this book is displayed in the following chart. The strategies fit into three categories:

- strategies for **connecting** new information with known information;
- strategies for **processing** new information;
- strategies for **transforming** or **personalizing** the new information.

When designing a lesson sequence, teachers determine their instructional purpose (connecting, processing, transforming, or personalizing), their content, and the strategy that best suits the purpose and content with student learning needs. We focus on active learning, planning for students who have different ways and rates of learning, and including individual and social learning opportunities.

LEARNING STRATEGIES FOR . . .

Connecting	Processing	Transforming/ Personalizing
Sort and Predict Building from Clues		
	Image-Cluster-Draft	Editing Without Agony
Think-of-a-Time	Carousel	
	Gallery Walk	Collaborative Summaries
	Listen-Sketch-Draft	
	ReQuest	
	Key Ideas and Questions	
	Thinking Bubbles	Concept Map
Anticipation Guide	Matching Thinking	
Frames: Quadrants...Concept Map...Collaborative Responses		

Sort and Predict—in collaborative groups, prior to presentation of new information, students explain their categorization of 20-30 teacher-chosen, key concept words.

Building from Clues—working collaboratively, prior to reading, students generate hypotheses and make connections among artifacts and language samples from the text.

Think-of-a-Time 1-2-3—using a focus question, students examine a concept from three points of view: as a participant, as a witness, and as a casual agent.

Carousel—students, in collaborative groups, generate and present group responses to individual data sets that, when grouped as a whole, represent the content to be studied.

Anticipation Guide—whole-class discussion centers around individual student responses to teacher-chosen key concepts from text.

Gallery Walk—students move in teams from collection to collection, responding with questions and records of new information.

Collaborative Summaries—students, working individually, generate key ideas before negotiating these in pairs and in groups of four—they are then ready to individually demonstrate their understanding.

Listen-Sketch-Draft—students sketch while text is being read; dialogue with a partner about the text, their sketch, and their thinking; then draft the key concepts of the passage.

ReQuest—using three kinds of questions (on the line, between the lines, beyond the lines), students work in teams to interact with the text.

Responding with Key Ideas and Questions—in pairs, students respond to text or another form of new information by synthesizing key ideas and then generating questions to be answered.

Thinking Bubbles—students represent their understanding in cartoon illustrations using the inside and outside voices of characters.

Concept Mapping—students, working together and then alone, identify key concepts in their learning and link these on a map using minimum language or sketched pictures.

Editing Without Agony—students draft criteria for powerful responses and work alone and collaboratively in successive drafts to personally achieve this criteria.

Image-Cluster-Draft—as the teacher reads an image of the context studied, students cluster what comes to their mind, prior to drafting their ideas.

Quadrants—students respond to information through the four quadrants of a thought: images, physical senses, emotions, and language.

Building Criteria—moving from a model of what works, students collaborate to establish a list of criteria to use when monitoring growth.

2

A Learning Focus

What would happen if students didn't have to come to school? How would we spend our time? These questions drive our practice. We believe that in the secondary school system, we can create a place where students *want* to be because they belong and because of the opportunities available to them for *learning*.

The Belief System

We operate from a fundamental set of beliefs. These beliefs guide the decisions we make in our classes:

- **all students can think and all students can learn to think more effectively.**

  The challenge we face as teachers is two-fold. First, many of our students no longer see themselves as capable learners. They have entered a spiral of descent where their actions or lack of actions virtually ensure limited success—inability to change or learn has become a self-fulfilling prophecy. The risks necessary in learning are too great. *How can we change student self-talk to be enabling, 'can do', or 'will risk'?*

  Second, many of our students learn in different ways, yet the learning situation in secondary schools has traditionally been unidimensional, that is, 'chalk and talk'. Many educators have learned to deliver 'good' lectures and feel competent with this strategy. While this may have been an effective learning strategy for us in school, it is unfortunately not an effective strategy for all learners and, indeed, often develops passivity in students. The lecture method is highly effective for covering content, but does not ensure that we *cover* the content with the learners. *How can we design learning sequences that develop different ways of thinking with content?*

- **learning requires active participation.**

  The social milieu of secondary classes does not always honor the principle of active learning. Many students have come to expect that it is the teacher's job to teach and the student's job to let it happen. Active involvement takes more energy—energy that some students are used to expending elsewhere. It may not be 'cool' to be active in the class. *How do we work to change the social milieu so that it values active participation?*

- **learning involves the social construction of knowledge.**
  The social or small group times in the class are *not* designed to
  make students better at regurgitating pieces of information.
  What is valued is the building of understanding, alone and
  with others. Adolescence is a social age when peer groups are
  of paramount importance. Students can and should learn to
  work responsibly in groups where the thinking of *all* group
  members is stretched beyond what it would have been had
  students worked as individuals. *How do we organize our classes
  for collaborative group learning experiences where students build
  understanding of the concepts and skills that are the content of the
  curriculum?*

- **diversity is prized.**
  Adolescence is also a time of sameness. To extend our learning
  and thinking, we need to shift the focus to one that values
  differences. Although we know that pattern making is common
  to our brains, each brain is unique. It is this uniqueness that
  enriches our interactions. *How do we orchestrate a learning
  environment where we are open to surprises in one another's thinking,
  and where we encounter and prize diversity rather than homogenity?*

- **questioning fuels new learning.**
  When we stop asking questions, we stop learning. This, too, is
  a shift in thinking. Powerful thinkers gain a strong foundation
  in a discipline and use this content knowledge to pose
  problems and search for solutions. We attempt to encourage
  students to develop their own questions and then to follow the
  lead of these questions. *Who asks the questions in our classes? Are
  these questions* real *questions that require a search or questions of
  recitation used for power and control?*

- **personal reflection linked to wise action supports growing
  independence in learning.**
  Reflecting helps make thinking explicit. Students and teachers
  reflect on changes in conceptual understanding and on how
  these changes came to be. This helps students accept
  responsibility for their learning. Reflecting is proactive in that
  what is learned through reflecting is then applicable information
  for use in other learning contexts. *Do we make time for reflection
  on learning? Do we reflect with our students on what and how we,
  too, are learning?*

- **the content of the curriculum is that worth knowing.**
  The decisions we make about *what* we teach are as important as
  the decisions we make about *how* we teach. Within the broad
  outlines of the curriculum, we extract key concepts, skills, and
  issues that will be important in the development of lifelong
  learners. These choices are made, when appropriate, with the
  students. We are able to justify the time that is spent

developing these understandings. *Is the content of our curriculum relevant to the learners and transferable to their lives and learning beyond the classroom? Can we connect the content to the lives of the learners in ways that make it worth knowing?*

- **interaction patterns in the classroom are based largely on student-student interaction.**
  The teacher's role is to extend and clarify understanding, to probe and question, and to provide experiences that encourage students to construct understanding. *Whose voice do we hear most in the classroom? Is this voice managing and informing or extending and clarifying?*

- **assessment and evaluation practices are intricately woven to instruction . . . and often are difficult to distinguish from instruction.**
  Evaluation is feedback on what is valued. As such, it is ongoing, individual, explicit, and designed to promote learning. Effective evaluation informs the practice of both the learners and the teacher—what instructional decision will most support learning? Ultimately, the key for evaluation practices is self-evaluation, that is, ''What do I next need to do?'' ''Who can help me?'' ''How will I know when I am getting better?'' Evaluation strategies, then, are based on criteria that is developed with the students in real learning situations. *How do we ensure that evaluation is driven by what is valued in our classroom and thus informs learning?*

If We Believe. . .	Then We Ask Ourselves These Questions. . .
• all students can think and all students can learn to think more effectively	• How can we change student self-talk to be enabling, 'can do', or 'will risk'? • How can we design learning sequences that develop different ways of thinking with content?
• learning requires active participation	• How do we work to change the social milieu so that it values active participation?
• learning involves the social construction of knowledge	• How do we organize our classes for collaborative group learning experiences where students build understandings of the concepts and skills that are the content of the curriculum?
• diversity is prized	• How do we orchestrate a learning environment where we are open to surprises in one another's thinking, and where we encourage and prize diversity rather than homogenity?
• questioning fuels new learning	• Who asks the questions in our classes? • Are these questions *real* questions that require a search or questions of recitation used for power and control?
• personal reflection linked to wise action supports growing independence in learning	• Do we make time for reflection on learning? • Do we reflect with our students on what and how we, too, are learning?
• the content of the curriculum is that worth knowing	• Is the content of our curriculum relevant to the learners and transferable to their lives and learning beyond the classroom? • Can we connect the content of the curriculum to the lives of the learners in ways that make it worth doing?
• interaction patterns in the classroom are based largely on student-student interactions	• Whose voice do we hear most in the classroom? • Is this voice managing and informing or extending and clarifying?
• assessment and evaluation practices are intricately woven to instruction and often are difficult to distinguish from instruction	• How do we ensure that evaluation is driven by what is valued in our classroom and thus informs learning?

Strategies

The use of thinking/learning strategies in our classrooms serves as the first step in the change process. Strategies give us different ways of working with our students and our curriculum. As we begin to work in different ways, we are better able to recognize and respond to differences in student learning. As our strategic repertoires increase, we make more informed choices about the strategies we use and fit them to our instructional goals and to students' needs. We shift from delivering the content of the curriculum to building it with our students, from teacher as technician to teacher as decision maker. We do not shift alone. The ultimate goal of thinking/learning strategies is that learners are better able to use the thinking behind the strategy in independent learning situations. Thus, they too develop the ability to choose from a strategic repertoire individually appropriate ways of connecting new information with known and so build understanding.

Working with strategies is akin to developing maps with students. Students get the picture of the territory to be covered, identify where they are going, learn different ways of getting there, decide when they are going alone, and when they are going together. Sometimes, we all go to the same place together. Ultimately, we can go to wherever we want on the map in a variety of ways. Choices grow rather than diminish.

It is the research of Howard Gardner (1985) that pushes our thinking on the "seven intelligences". These ways are summarized as follows:

Verbal/Linguistic: thinking in words and languages

Logical/
Mathematical: thinking in patterns and numbers, inductively
                       and deductively

Visual/Spatial: thinking visually, creating images

Body/Kinesthetic: thinking through motion and body sense

Musical/Rhythmic: thinking through tones, sounds, rhythm, and
                       beat

Interpersonal: thinking through communication and
                       relationships with people

Intrapersonal: thinking metacognitively about oneself and
                       one's thinking

Gardner states that each person has all seven intelligences. However, each person develops these differently, resulting in unique thinking patterns. Each person has the capability to further develop *all* seven ways of thinking. They allow us to pose problems, to solve problems, and can enhance learning in the school curriculum and beyond the school walls.

Considering the complexity of ways of learning, we use strategies to link learners with the content of the curriculum. In order to support diversity among learners and to extend individual ways of thinking, strategies must share several key attributes. Each strategy:

- **is constructive for all individuals.**
  Strategies must enable the building of understanding whether alone, in small groups, or extended throughout the learning community of the class. They must be open enough to invite personal construction using prior knowledge, experience, new information, and understanding. They are not based on one right answer or one right way.

- **is supportive of risk taking.**
  Strategies help build a climate of mutual respect, support, and trust. Diversity is honored. Setting individual goals and stepping into our individual unknowns is a challenge we all attempt to grasp.

- **focuses on the development of social skills.**
  Within a strategy, there is room for the novice and the expert to work together in a mutually supportive way. The expectation and the practice is such that all students learn to work effectively in groups where the learning of all is enhanced by the group interaction. This requires the explicit instruction in social skills, as well as in cognitive skills.

- **includes reflection and feedback to ensure personal adaptation and transfer to different contexts.**
  There is no one right way to work with a strategy. Building in ongoing cycles of reflection on the utility of the strategy helps learners extend and adapt the process for use in other situations and contexts, both in and out of the classroom. Common questions include: ''How is this helping you learn?'', ''What do you notice about your thinking?'', and ''How will you change this next time?''

- **strengthens with practice.**
  Strategies are not one-shot events. Teachers and students become more competent with the strategy over time and thus are more able to adapt and integrate it into their personal learning repertoires.

* adapted from ''The Art of Strategic Connections'', Brownlie (1992)

As mentioned, our goal in working with the strategies is to move students toward independent application of the thinking behind the strategy—to extend their ways of knowing. With this end in mind, teachers model both the strategy in a variety of contexts and the thinking behind the strategy—the steps they have chosen and why they have chosen them. Both the purpose and the process are thus shared with the students. The steps in the following chart have been effective in this process.

SETTING THE STAGE
1. Identify the strategy to be taught.
2. Discuss the reasons why it is being taught.
3. Tell the steps of the strategy.

MODELING AND DIRECT INSTRUCTION
4. Teach the strategy in an appropriate context.
5. Provide opportunities for whole-group work, collaborative-group work, and individual work.
6. Reflect with your students on what you did and why.

GUIDING PRACTICE
7. Review the steps of the strategy with the students.
8. Establish criteria for effective use of the strategy.
9. Use the strategy in a variety of contexts and with a variety of texts.
10. Reflect with the students on their growing competency with the strategy.

ENCOURAGING INDEPENDENT APPLICATION
11. Provide opportunities for students to use the strategy independently in materials of their own choosing.
12. Encourage adaptation of the strategy to fit text, context, and personal style.
13. Monitor the students' expertise and independent application of the strategy.
14. Monitor the gradual diminishment of teacher support needed.

From *Tomorrow's Classroom Today*. F. Brownlie, S. Close & L. Wingren, Pembroke Publishers, 1990.

This models the ongoing instruction/evaluation link, what we know informs what we do, and the cycle continues.

This learning is a journey. We are enjoying our explorations, and invite you to join us. We think you will enjoy our traveling if you continually search for new ways to arrive at your destination. We would delight in hearing the connections you make, and the possibilities you uncover in your practice. Collaboration enriches us all!

3

Sort and Predict

Whether we are explicitly learning or simply experiencing events, becoming aware of the categories we use—and revising them whenever we choose—is the key to being able to analyze a subject, synthesize new insights about it, and evaluate how suitable something is for our purpose.

— R. Gross, *Peak Learning*

Sometimes students seek to make connections by searching for information; other times, connections come as they explore ways of organizing knowledge and experience. Some connections develop through collaboration and exploratory dialogue; others, through self-exploration and reflection.

— Ministry of Education and Ministry Responsible for Multiculturalism and Human Rights, *Thinking in the Classroom, Volume 1*

Advance organizers are important to concept formation; they provide an anchor where information and ideas received during the instructional period can be attached . . .

— D. Sanders & J. Sanders, *Teaching Creativity Through Metaphor*

There must be time for reflection, synthesis, evaluation, organization and reorganization. Without this, teachers and students alike are swept away in a torrent of information which is not effectively owned or made meaningful.

— M. McLaren, *The Search for Understanding*

The grade nine social studies class noisily entered the room. We had planned an active strategy to introduce them to the next focus of study, aiming to keep them involved and on task, during this, the last period of the week.

TEACHER: Our goal in today's class is two-fold: we want to introduce a strategy that is new to you, and we want to use the strategy to get you thinking about our next major curriculum focus —British Columbia as it prepares to join Confederation. You will have noticed that we have a team of observers today. Since they are interested in your thinking, in getting to know you better, and in the impact of this strategy on your learning, please begin by writing your name and date on a piece of paper that we will be able to take away with us. Now, would you write and tell us what you do well in school and why you think this is so.

The group quickly settled in, jotting down personal successes in school. They seemed surprised at this request, but all generated a response.

GREG: I like to do Metalwork, woodwork, and automechanics (shops courses). My whole family is really mechanically inclined and has good brains so it just runs in the family (skill).

NATASHA: I do very well in social studies because I enjoy it and I love History.

MATHEW: Non-structured creative writing. The reason I do this one thing well (to quote you) is because I enjoy it.

ERIN: One thing I do really well in school is my ability to complete and do my homework and assignments. I am a determined perfectionist. I feel I have to do well in everything. However, one subject I do well in and find very easy is math. I think I do well in math because it is exact and it has order; therefore, I know the answer is either wrong or right.

This range of responses reminds us of the diversity in the student groups. One integrated special-needs student worked with a teacher's assistant who could script her language. Two ESL students had limited fluency in English. We had a mixed group—students who preferred independence, choice, and little structure to students preferring tight order and clearly defined right and wrong answers. As well, we had students who liked writing and content, while others preferred hands-on, practical courses. Our strategies would need to welcome and support the learning of all students.

Set a purpose for the lesson.

Acknowledge the visiting teachers and their role in the class.

The more we know about the diversity of the learners, the more able we are to teach them.

TEACHER: Today we will work in groups. These groups should be comprised of two or three members. Make eye contact with someone you would like to work with. If they have returned eye contact and you can arrange yourselves in twenty seconds, you can choose your own partners.

I was impressed with the silence of this choosing. Everyone quickly connected with at least one other person and was ready for the next step.

TEACHER: OK. Anyone need help finding a partner? Then move quickly. . . . Great. You sure can hustle when given choices! Before I give you the worksheet, I have another reflection for you. We have had some difficulty in making our group work productive. Since you have had the choice in partners today, I hope that this may keep you on task. Would you also take a moment and reflect in writing about whether or not you think your group work today will be productive for you.

GREG: Yes, I think I will be able to work with my partner.

NATASHA: No.

MATHEW: Personally, I think that varied input greatly increases the ability to clearly perceive all sides of an objective.

ERIN: Yes, working with the partner will help my learning, and I think that we will most likely drive the teachers crazy!

TEACHER: Thank you. This strategy is called *Sort and Predict*. I will give each group or partnership a worksheet. On this worksheet are about twenty-five words. These words are all taken from the chapter ''British Columbia: From Colonies to Confederation''. Your task is to sort these words into five categories and then to label the categories. Your challenge is to make one of these categories unique from all other categories chosen by other groups. Try to make it defensible, too! As you prepare your categories, think about what you know already about the concepts and ideas presented, and ways that would make sense in connecting them. Think also about what you might expect to discover in a chapter that included all these words. Feel free to rip or cut the words apart or to rewrite them.

As the teacher handed out the sheets, the students quickly began reading over the words and talking about possibilities for the categories. Most preferred to cut or rip them apart, although several groups left the sheet intact and began writing their categories.

Small groups create increased opportunity for interaction.

Responsibility for productive use of time is a responsibility of all members of the class, not just of the teacher.

Emphasis is on individual accountability within the group or partnership.

A unique category stretches thinking and decreases noise levels.

Hudson Bay Company	resources	1849
timber	trading	coal
British Columbia	1858	isolation
George Simpson	Crown Colony	USA
gold	negotiations	fur
49th parallel	54 40'	governor
Oregon Territory	annexation	Russia
Columbia River	James Polk	Fort Langley
Oregon Boundary	Treaty Fort	Vancouver

The students worked for fifteen minutes. They constructed categories, and negotiated and debated about connections, relevance, and ways to out-think the other students with their unique category. Categories changed frequently during this period. The teacher moved among the student groups, listening and occasionally asking for clarification of items in a category. I was impressed with the apparent on-task behavior and the amount of interaction within the student groups.

TEACHER: This is a two-minute warning. Try to wrap up your discussion within the next couple of minutes. Be prepared to defend your categories to us.

There was a last flurry of activity.

TEACHER: Let's begin by hearing some of the unique categories you chose. As we listen, we will give you a 'thumbs up' if we do not have a similar category, a 'thumbs waving across' if we are not sure and need to ask you a question, or a 'thumbs down' if your category is not unique. Notice that these are silent thumbs. Only one group has the floor. Your ticket to speak is either to share your unique category or to ask a question of the speaker. Please tell us your category name and the words included in the category. Sean, do you want to be first?

SEAN: British Columbia was a Crown Colony, not in the USA, and had the Columbia River, the Hudson Bay Company, Fort Langley, and Fort Vancouver in it. It's a sentence! That's the category name.

Many of the students groaned, but after several complaints of "You never told us we could write a sentence" and "Is that a fair category?", Sean and his partners received a 'thumbs up'. They grinned broadly.

TEACHER: First time lucky, I guess. I would predict, however, that next time we try this *Sort and Predict*, making a sentence may no longer be unique. Who else is ready?

GREG: Our title is 'Negotiations' and the words in it are 54 40', Russia, Oregon Boundary Treaty, USA, annexation, 49th parallel, James Polk, Oregon Territory, and isolation. They all had to do with negotiating being part of Canada.

Support is provided as necessary. Informed instruction can grow from these opportunities for listening in on meaning making.

Two-minute warning respects the learners' needs for closure.

Listeners have a role, extending the categories beyond the original group of students.

Silent thumbs encourage response without interference.

Fewer teacher rules invite definition or rules made by the students, as necessary.

Greg and his partner had several 'wavering thumbs' but no other group had exactly the same words under 'Negotiations'. Several groups expressed surprise at being able to use a word as a category name. Again, they were reminded of how few rules had been given.

MATHEW: Ours is really unique. It is 'words which share letters with the word 'platypus', can't brush your teeth with it, or is found in the dictionary.

Before Mathew could read his list, he and his group had received a resounding 'thumbs down'.

STUDENTS: That's three titles.

That sounds to me like they panicked when the time was running out.

I want to know what their other categories were.

The humor was infectious. Mathew and his group are students who are known to their classmates as those who always push the boundaries. The teacher smiled at them and suggested they had just been caught. Next time, they would have to work a little harder at convincing the others of their uniqueness within the constraints of the task. They returned her smile and said, "No problem."

TEACHER: Before this class ends, please do three things.

1. Record the categories you have created.

2. Reflect again, commenting on what you noticed about how you worked and how this strategy affected your learning. If you have advice on how to make this lesson more effective, give yourself permission to add that, too.

3. Look back at the words in your categories. Please mark any word that you would not be able to talk about in detail. These will be the concepts that you use to guide your independent reading in the next class.

Students practice personal record keeping after collaborative group work.

Students reflect on process and content, and opportunity for decision making in the instructional process.

The students returned to their independent tasks. Their reflections included:

GREG: I worked as good as I thought we would. I learnt the meaning of annexation. We did awesome. I wouldn't change a thing. Made you think.

NATASHA: Did great.

MATHEW: I think I learned more than I might've by myself, simply from seeing other minds at work; it allows a clearer view of human nature. As for what I learned, well, I didn't actually know there was an Oregon Boundary Treaty.

ERIN: I feel that I worked very well with my partner. We had a few disagreements; however, we bounced ideas off of each other which resulted in better ideas! The class noise was also not very loud, and it felt like quite a comfortable atmosphere. Most of the words in the exercise were review. Some of the words I recognized and reviewed their meaning/ importance from history. Other people also reviewed their meanings when we were having the oral discussion.

*These were the categories that Erin and her partner identified. The words with the * are those Erin felt she would not be able to talk about in depth.*

Number Group: 1858, 1849, 49th parallel, 54 40'*

Family Compact
   Group: isolation, crown colony, governor, negotiations*

Resources Group: resources, timber, fur, coal, gold, Russia*

The "Pair" Group: Oregon Territory, Oregon Boundary Treaty, George Simpson, James Polk*

Unique Group: British Columbia

The final bell rang and the class was dismissed. We were all surprised at how quickly the hour had passed and how involved the students had been with one another and with linking the content of the curriculum.

The Next Class

The students were prepared for a more individual/independent task when they returned. They read the next chapter in their book independently and collected information on the words/concepts that they had identified as being less familiar to them. They then re-categorized the original words in categories that would make sense based on what they had just read. Some students chose to complete this re-categorization alone, while others chose to work with their groups. Sometimes these words are not re-categorized, but are used to make a *Concept Map,* reflecting a personal understanding of what is read.

Cross-Curricular Applications

1. *Home Economics*
   In a chapter on interfacing, the students were given key words to sort into categories, and asked to choose one unique category,

label all categories, and predict questions they might need to have answered as they read the information in the text. One of the groups chose as their most unique category, *love*. Their words included 'adhesive', 'bond', 'interfacing', 'interwoven', 'connect', 'glue', 'dominant', 'texture'. They had no questions on this category.

2. *Law*

   Students brainstormed current issues. These issues became the words or data base for *Sort and Predict*. In an attempt to increase awareness of the issues at hand, students worked in teams to classify the issues. No set number of groups was given. Once the classifications were completed, they were shared among the class members. Individual students then created a bumper sticker for their 'most important issue'.

   One group of students created the following list:

pollution	oil — lack of	AIDS
natural disaster	drugs	racism
drift-net fishing	ozone layer	human rights
overpopulation	animal extinction	suicide
dictatorship	rape	oil spills
alcohol abuse	smoking	malnutrition
water preservation	garbage	cancer
drunk driving	gangs	war
heart disease	dishonesty	hunger
greenhouse effect	illiteracy	nuclear war
child abuse	lack of recycling	injustice
unemployment	pesticides/chemicals	Mid-East crisis
natural resources — lack of	rain forest destruction	overlogging

3. *ESL Language*

   Students worked with partners to categorize the following English idioms, explain their categories, and generate questions about what they needed to know. Much discussion grew from this strategy.

   as light as a feather
   as dry as a bone
   The toddler was a clinging vine near his mother.
   The mountain of paper work seemed to grow.
   John's head is a computer.
   laughed like a hyena
   bright like the sun
   as busy as a bee
   as quick as a wink
   His heart is an iceberg.
   soft like silk
   cheeks like roses
   eyes like stars
   Her heart is a fountain of kindness.
   as stubborn as a mule

Ann is a walking encyclopedia.
A fossil of a man greeted us at the door.
loud like thunder
worked like a horse
Mr. Mather's bark is worse than his bite.
as cold as ice
as sweet as honey
as white as snow
as lovely as a rose
The army of ants attacked the fallen lollipop.

4. *Science*

The students were given the following data set. Prior to studying the chapter, their task was to classify the chemicals and establish criteria for their classification. This manipulation of data helped the students make their own connections, formulate questions, and extend their connections through the study.

HCl	SOz	Pbl_2	CH_4	CO
N_2O_5	H_2	$AgNO_3$	H_2O	SiF_4
$FeCL_3$	$PbSO_4$	HNO_3	Rbl	Cal_2
HgO	C_8H_{18}	XeF_6	NO_2	C_2H_5OH
CO_2	$CuSO_4$	$NaCl$	S_8	CCl_4
N_2	$FeCl_2$	C_6H_6	$NaOH$	$CaCl_2$
KBr	NH_3	$NaHCO_3$	K_2CrOu	$KClO_3$
O_2	$COCL_2 \cdot 6H_2O$			

Annette's reflection in her learning log demonstrates the importance of this kind of strategy in matching the learning needs of a diverse student population.

> Today's activity, classification, was quite interesting. Our group worked very cooperatively and discussed many ideas, concepts, and questions. We got along very well and basically agreed on almost everything. If we did not we just discussed everyone's opinion, and their reasoning behind it. I think that I learned a lot more than I can say because I'm sure that in the future I will be able to say "That's right. I remember that from the classification activity." I really enjoyed this activity and I think that making us find the answers ourselves rather than giving them to us is much better.

5. *English*

Prior to reading the short story "The Two Sisters" by Pauline Johnson, students sorted words into five groups, labelled the groups, created a unique group, and predicted about the upcoming story. These are the words they sorted:

daughters	Peace	peaks	shrouded
Tyee	canyon	glories	Capilanos
torrent	opals	Pale-faces	
Brotherhood	coast	immovable	
potlatch	dream-hills	festoon	

After reading the story, they regrouped the words to show an understanding of the story.

SORT AND PREDICT

1. Choose twenty to thirty key concept words from a text.

2. Arrange students in partnerships or small groups.

3. Ask students to categorize the words in five categories and create one unique category.

4. Students label the categories.

5. Share the categories among the groups, beginning with the 'unique' group.

6. The audience listens to give feedback on whether or not the category is indeed 'unique'.

7. Individually, students identify words that they need more information on in order to be able to talk about them with clarity.

8. Conclude the lesson with student reflection on:
   • personal effectiveness in the group;
   • expectations for success;
   • the impact of the group and the activity on learning;
   • what they need to know next.

4

Building from Clues

Students of science . . . clearly need higher-order thinking skills. These skills are qualitative and related to processing and using information in ways that suggest a path for effective action.

— P. DeHart Hurd, *Why We Must Transform Science Education*

Understanding . . . is more a matter of what people do than something they have . . . when people show these actions, then, we see evidence that they understand something.

— D. Perkins, *Educating for Insight*

In order for optimum learning to occur, students should think about what they already know about a topic, be presented with new information, and through the mediation process, gradually come to understand the topic.

— D. Pearson et al., *Developing Expertise in Reading Comprehension: What should be taught?*

Ultimately, we want students to grow to be independent. For them to do that, they have to have a sense of what the criteria is that makes them successful. For a long time, the criteria has been a mystery to students. Part of the spirit is inviting students to help develop the criteria so that they know exactly what they have to work toward to be successful.

— R. Tierney, M. Carter & L. Desai, *Portfolio Asessment in the Reading-Writing Classroom*

Prior to this class, the grade ten science students had collected what they thought they knew about acid rain, generated and categorized related questions, and offered a range of hypotheses. This lesson begins an indepth investigation. The students will analyze, interpret, and evaluate the causes, effects, and implications of acid rain. At the end of the study, they will demonstrate their findings and justify their recommendations to a range of community stakeholders.

TEACHER: At the end of last class we talked about the acid rain study. I invited you to begin gathering information and to anticipate how scientists might approach this kind of investigation. What might a scientist consider as she or he begins to probe? Discuss your ideas with your partner.

The students talked in pre-arranged pairs, sharing possibilities. The teacher said, "five," and in just short of five seconds, the voices disappeared. He pointed to a raised hand. It was obvious this class was comfortable with partner interaction and collective sharing of understanding.

MARCO: Scientists probably think about who could help them.

TEACHER: Thank you, someone else . . .

He acknowledged and valued each person's response.

STUDENTS: Questions. They'd have lots of unanswered questions.

I think they know a lot and enjoy what they do.

I think experts know who to contact because they would know where problems are and they'd know who else is working on them.

They'd be looking out for information to help them. They might keep files.

Someone would be uncovering the problems and some would be working on solutions.

TEACHER: Today's strategy, *Building from Clues*, allows you to use many kinds of thinking that scientific experts might use. I will present six clues: two are experiments you will observe, one is a visual that I will place on the overhead projector, and three are short passages from your science textbook. After each clue is presented, you will have a few minutes to discuss and jot down connections with your partner. We will stop and listen to your connections. When all of the clues have been discussed, you and your partner will design a prediction that includes the major concepts you determined from the clues. This is an opportunity for you to create a powerful way to show your understanding about

Content is selected and organized once student prior knowledge is established.

The teacher is setting the stage for practising expert behavior.

Link elements of the process to collaborative and individual responses.

acid rain. You will have fifteen minutes to prepare your draft. After this, we will observe a few presentations to build criteria for powerful responses. You will then present to one other group and they will give you feedback.

Building criteria makes explicit to the students the attributes of a powerful response.

As a whole group, we will add details to the criteria for powerful responses before you and your partner assess your draft. For next class, you will take the clues and construct your own personal draft. You will have an opportunity to present it to three other students.

Evaluation feedback is ongoing. The feedback cycle supports growth and change.

He wrote the sequence on the overhead.

1. Examine clues
2. Create a collaborative presentation
3. Listen to presentations and develop criteria
4. Present to one group and listen to detailed feedback
5. Listen and offer feedback
6. Self-assess
7. Prepare own version, from clues, for the next class

Frame the teaching plan.

TEACHER: *Building from Clues* offers opportunities to expand the use of our many intelligences. Before we begin, take a quick reading on the developing capacities of your seven intelligences. Feel free to talk to your partner if you wish.

Build an investigation in developing capacities or self-knowledge as a motivation.

The students opened their binders to a graph and in less than three minutes had given themselves a numerical rating. The teacher walked around listening to individual responses.

Developing Intelligences

	1 2 3 4 5 undeveloped highly developed		
Seven Intelligences	**What I know about myself**	**What I noticed today**	**Advice for next time**
Verbal/Linguistic			
Logical/Mathematical			
Visual/Spatial			
Musical/Rhythmic			
Body/Kinesthetic			
Interpersonal			
Intrapersonal			

TEACHER: As we work through the process today, notice your skills within each of the intelligences. You'll be reflecting and offering yourself advice at the end of the class. Turn your paper over and use the back to collect data as you gain information from the clues.

The teacher had set up two stations with litmus paper and two bottles of clear liquid. One bottle was labelled 1985 and the other 1992.

TEACHER: In clue number one, bring forward all that you know about pH. Move so you can observe. You have a minute to talk about pH . . . Before you are two strips of litmus paper. We will place drops of lake water from 1985 on paper A and drops of lake water from 1992 on paper B. Observe what happens, then talk to your partner.

Informed discussion distributes knowledge gained in previous classes.

TEACHER: What connections did you make?

STUDENTS: 1985 pH was 4 and 1992 pH was 2.

There was less acid in the water in 1985 than in 1992.

TEACHER: Does anyone have a hypothesis about this?

A number of students offered hypotheses. The teacher pressed for substantiation and elaboration of positions.

The teacher's role is to help connect, clarify, and extend student understanding.

TEACHER: Any questions formulating?

STUDENTS: I wonder if that is local water because if it is, I'm going to be worried.

What does acid level do to us when we swim in it or drink it?

The teacher elicited questions and invited the inquirers to be thinking about a question they might pursue in their own personal investigation. He often invited his students to shape their independent work, offering many opportunities for application and extension of a repertoire of strategies learned.

Curriculum content develops from student questions within a content framework.

TEACHER: Second clue . . .

He held up two beakers that each contained a rock.

TEACHER: Position yourselves to observe and talk. I will pour an acid on each rock. Notice the reaction.

". . . memory retrieval is enhanced when recall is multimodal" McKim (1990)

He poured vinegar on the rocks as observers watched intently. Puzzled looks turned slowly into dialogue.

TEACHER: Five . . . What did you notice?

The teacher networked the observations, thanking each person who responded.

STUDENTS: Smells like vinegar

Smells like 7-Up

Bubbling, fizzing around limestone rock

Acid fizzes cause it's eating away at the rock

TEACHER: You have two clues. What connections are you making?

STUDENTS: Acid water eats out rock. Over time statues or stone buildings could disintegrate if rain was like the 1992 water.

It is easier to work with others on these things. I thought totally different about things.

The teacher placed a transparency on the overhead projector.

TEACHER: Study the visual and talk again.

The students talked, pointing at elements. One girl's face grimaced as she explained her understandings. As observers, we noticed the on-task behavior of all students.

". . . the more students can talk about what they are doing . . . the greater the learning." Caine and Caine (1991)

TEACHER: Five.

Hands shot up. The girl with the grimace responded angrily.

STUDENTS: That rain is like the lake water and it will eventually ruin our community. People won't want to live here because taxes will have to go up to pay for repairs.

I still wonder what it's doing to us.

Nods of contempt showed growing understanding of concepts.

TEACHER: What's your hypothesis?

KIM: My cousin told me the valley is like a collection depot for pollutants. He said some researchers are investigating certain diseases and their related causes. So far, their results are scary. I want to know if it is better to live in another part of the lower mainland.

Content is embedded in life-like experiences that require genuine interactions.

Attentive listening reflected serious consideration of the question.

TEACHER: I will reveal each of the remaining clues quite quickly. Talk again, and jot down any details you think will help you.

The teacher uncovered the passage.

''Acid rain is strong enough to erode exposed metal surface and eat away stone statues and even limestone buildings.''

TEACHER: Five. (pointing to the first hand up)

STUDENTS: Wind pushes pollution into the valley and goes back by the lakes which is a cycle.

The acid rain flows from the rivers back to the ocean.

City pollution is the problem. It's like a chain reaction. Pollution released from factories is blown into the valley. Clouds become full of chemicals then acid rain falls into the rivers and kills off the fish and the water flows back to the city.

TEACHER: Thank you. Here is clue five.

''Acid rain causes chemical changes in soil and water bodies that, over many years, can reduce soil fertility, retard tree growth, and kill fish and plant life.''

The students related new ideas to their base of knowledge. Aspects of this complex issue were contemplated and ideas were expanded as they reached to express sophisticated understandings. The teacher invited responses again by saying, ''five''.

STUDENTS: When water is polluted, it affects all.

Growth is harmed because water is needed for growth.

TEACHER: Last clue. As I tell you about it, think of original ways to present your ideas. You will be summarizing, or pulling your ideas together, and presenting them to show your understandings.

"Every year people die of emphysema, lung cancer, or bronchitis. In cities such as Los Angeles, there is an increase in respiratory ailments on days when the air pollution index is high."

TEACHER: What strikes you now?

Connections to their own lives emerged first. One girl, visibly moved by the passage, said, "It's like we live in a giant cigarette." The teacher asked for further connections.

STUDENTS: People inhale poison into their systems and diseases follow.

The cycle is in action again. People will get sick many ways, through the air and by eating polluted fish. It will slowly damage everything and cost a lot of money.

Every system will be affected. Economics, personal health, and the way we live.

This makes me mad. I'm breathing air that I can't handle. I'm mad that it's being polluted without my permission.

TEACHER: You've had six clues. You've collected some data to help you. Now your task is to create an individual presentation to demonstrate what you know about acid rain.

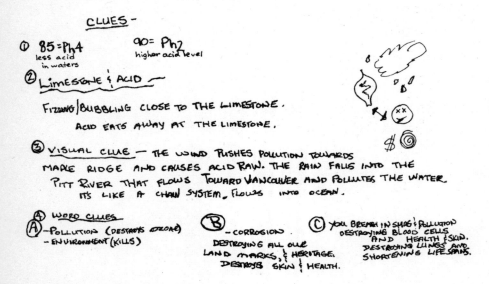

STUDENTS: Can we write something?

TEACHER: Of course. The response can be in any form you can create in fifteen minutes, using materials in the room—press releases, political cartoons, documentaries, interviews, and sketches. Play with possibilities like we've done in the past. We'll stop in five minutes to hear what you're planning.

The students worked in partners weighing, formulating, and negotiating shared meaning. After five minutes, they stopped to hear possibilities. A poem, a scene from a hospital room of the future, and a real estate commercial were taking shape. Students not yet committed to a form for their demonstrations seemed more comfortable after seeing other people's ideas unfold.

Modeling possibilities fuels thinking.

TEACHER: What did you notice about each of the presentations?

STUDENTS: They're certainly different.

Yeah! I'm impressed at how quickly the ideas come together. Once we decided on a way to go, the ideas just boiled.

TEACHER: What makes a successful partnership? Talk to your partner about what you did to pull your ideas together. What did you have to do?

Developing criteria builds successful engagement with process.

The students reflected with each other. Some shrugged their shoulders and said, "I don't know." Others began "First we . . . then . . ." conversations. After one minute, the teacher started a list on the board.

TEACHER: What did you have to do to make your partnership work?

STUDENTS: Work on ideas together.

Look for things we both agreed on.

Do a lot of talking.

Work through feeling confused.

Everyone laughed, nodding and reflecting on the hard work they had engaged in to create ways to show their understanding. The teacher quickly pressed them to identify key elements of powerful partnerships.

A list was generated.

Building criteria for content, process, and product knowledge is integral to the learning sequence.

1. Listen to each other and respond.
2. Show respect for the other person's ideas.
3. Build on each other's ideas.
4. Be willing to throw out some ideas and try new ones.
5. Reach agreement.

TEACHER: You have about ten minutes to work on your presentations.

After a generous ten minutes, the class stopped to watch a number of presentations. The students were instructed to watch for powerful use of the content clues. After each presentation, the students identified specifics that gave power to the draft.

The teacher listed the developing criteria on the chalkboard:

- organized and focused
- ideas flowed
- points explained with details
- humor used purposefully
- believable
- original ways of presenting facts
- detailed, accurate information

The students were sitting in groups of four at lab tables. The teacher invited each pair to present to the closest set of partners and to notice powerful attributes in the response.

Acid Rain

The air is full of smoke
Pollution everywhere
There once was a beautiful earth
Now there's nothing there
We have nothing left, but it's all our fault
We did it to ourselves.

The plants and the trees
The fish in the seas
We did it to them, too.

Mihaela

TEACHER: Look at our criteria. Did you notice any other attributes that need to be included?

Four were added:

> - word choice created strong images
> - problem solved in a thoughtful way
> - all facts included
> - short and to the point

TEACHER: With your partner, assess your response using the criteria. Was yours powerful, competent, developing, or undeveloped?

The students assessed their presentations, articulating evidence for their assessment category. The teacher concluded the class with a reflection.

TEACHER: Your homework is to make a personal design using these clues. Take a minute to jot down ideas for making your presentation powerful. Look back at your intelligences graph. Notice any changes and give yourself advice for the next time.

The class ended with individuals showing changes they had noticed in the use of their intelligences.

Categories adapted from Reading and Responding by Jeroski, Brownlie & Kaser (1991)

Developing Intelligences

	1 2 3 4 5
	undeveloped highly developed

Seven Intelligences	What I know about myself		What I noticed today	Advice for next time
Verbal/Linguistic	4^+	5	I noticed that I have all these talents that I have never used and I feel better being able to use them. We came out with bigger words to express the way we feel.	Listen even better. Give more information
Logical/Mathematical	3	5		
Visual/Spatial	5	5^+		
Musical/Rhythmic	5	5		
Body/Kinesthetic	2	4		
Interpersonal	2	5^x		
Intrapersonal	5	4^-		

The Next Class

A number of individuals presented their personal designs. Criteria for powerful presentation of the curriculum clues were refined. The students moved back into their groups of four to present individually. Listeners offered feedback. Students assessed their presentations, offering evidence for their category choice (powerful, competent, developing, or undeveloped).

The class sorted and categorized vocabulary from a newspaper article and developed more specific predictions about the effects of acid rain. With a partner, they read the article and searched for key ideas. The teacher worked with the class to create a cluster on the overhead projector. The class ended with individual writing to show their present knowledge.

Cross-Curricular Applications

1. *Social Studies*

   A set of slides, pictures, artifacts, or revealing pieces of text can be used to generate hypotheses before or during a sequence.

   In a Pacific Rim unit, the teacher showed six artifacts. The students composed predictions for elements of the culture before beginning the study.

   In a First Nations study, a set of eight quotations were revealed. The students composed collaborative and individual stories using key ideas from the quotes. They self-assessed.

   - I am satisfied with what I have done because it kept my attention while I was reading it. I noticed that my brain was really working through the whole thing.

   - My ending is very moving. I noticed I am finally using my brain and can use powerful words.

   - mine is powerful because it had a lesson and I showed how the First Nation's people respect nature. I noticed that I really pushed myself! Great job.

   - I feel satisfied because I'm happy with what I wrote. I noticed that thinking about it wasn't really that hard. At first I thought I was going to strain my brain.

2. *Math*

   Elements of a problem were revealed. The students had to generate and solve a full problem using the clues.

3. *Environmental Studies*

Phrases from an environmental news fax were revealed and responded to. The students collaboratively constructed, presented, and defended elements of an issue before developing their individual hypotheses.

SET OF PHRASES

- London Rainforest Action Group
- London-based arms dealer U.S.I.
- contract value US $60 million
- the cream of Liberian forests
- threatened biological resource
- novel variation on the debt for nature
- an arms for logging concession swap

Concept: Relation of people to environment
Sub-Concept: Global Rainforest Destruction

BUILDING FROM CLUES

1. Students are grouped in partners.

2. Students reflect on how scientists problem solve.

3. The teacher presents five or six clues, one at a time.

4. After each presentation of a clue, partners make connections, question, and predict.

5. Partners compose a theory (hypothesis, prediction, explanation, presentation, story) that covers all of the clues.

6. Criteria can be developed for powerful partnerships, and students assess their partnership skills.

BUILDING CRITERIA

1. Students present their collaborative theories *or* use a published writing sample from text.

2. Students listen to presentation of theories and notice powerful elements or 'what works'.

3. As a class, generate a list of criteria, i.e., powerful elements.

4. In groups of four, one pair of students presents to a second pair. Listeners offer feedback on powerful elements using the criteria developed.

5. As a class, refine developing criteria.

6. Partners assess their own presentations, based on personally prioritized criteria.

7. Each student gives himself or herself advice for their next personal working experience and reflects on what she or he noticed about his or her learning in this process.

8. Students write a personal theory.

9. Students are grouped in teams of four. Each student presents his or her theory of the group for feedback based on chosen criteria.
   Feedback pattern is PQS:
   • praise — what works
   • question — I wonder
   • suggestion — you might consider (Elbow, 1982)

10. Student self-assesses and sets a new learning goal.

11. Criteria are posted and visible.

12. Refinement of criteria is ongoing to fit purpose, audience, and form.

5

Think-of-a-Time/ Carousel

... personal storytelling ... usually sets in motion a sequence of stories ... If you analyze a sequence of this kind you will almost always discover that, far from being a random collection, they constitute an endeavor to reach a collective understanding of some important theme ...

— H. Rosen, *Why is the narrative story so important to children in their journey to become literate?*

Students generate more ideas in collaborative settings ... students have more incidental and planned opportunities to use language as an instrument of learning. Students can learn to recognize that their own experience and thoughts are of value when they are learning new information.

— J. Reid, P. Forrestal & J. Cook, *Small Group Learning in the Classroom*

Hearing different points of view, the clash of minds, the exchange of ideas, and the listing of problems and their solutions all contribute to the development of thinking skills and deeper levels of understanding.

— S. Hill & T. Hill, *The Collaborative Classroom*

Collaborative learning ... where more emphasis is placed on the types of cooperation and communication ... needed in an information age ... may have several effects:
(1) making classrooms more success-oriented;
(2) counteracting ... social isolation ...;
(3) building oral language skills by teaching structured ways of talking together about what is being learned ...

— J. Healy, *Endangered Minds*

The grade ten students know a team of teachers will be observing the learning sequence. They are visibly anxious as twelve adults move to the back of the room. There are whispers of acknowledgement between the partners as they greet the teachers.

TEACHER: Good afternoon. You are right. For the first time, we have guests with us. Let's talk about why a team of educators would participate in a lesson with us.

The students were seated in triads. They turned to their groups and a flood of conversation released the tension.

STUDENTS: You told us you were learning some new ways of teaching with other teachers.

You are being evaluated.

They came in to see how we work in groups.

Maybe they came to see how much we improved!

A few giggles erupted. Knowing looks permeated the room. The teacher laughed and commented to the observers on how resistant the class had been to any new approach to learning. She talked about her uncertainties and her reasons for persevering. The class was absolutely silent as she talked about why she had been expanding her ways of teaching and how determined she had had to be to get them to be more flexible.

Information is shared with all participants in a community of learners.

TEACHER: Our observers will share with us their reflections before they leave. We are about to immerse ourselves in a study of communication. You will notice how you are developing complex understandings as we move through a learning sequence over the next three classes. By using a variety of strategies or approaches to learning, you will be able to demonstrate and assess your understandings in powerful ways.

The teacher placed a familiar planning sheet on the overhead projector.

Connecting	Processing	Transforming/ Personalizing
Think-of-a-Time • critical elements of effective conversations **Carousel** • to summarize elements of effective conversations	**Carousel to Process** • twelve blocks to listening • newspaper	**Collaborative Summary** • to present findings in a press release

She walked the students through the plan and outlined its goals.

TEACHER: We have been talking about our own learning and our own capacities. I was reading Robert Fulghum's book last night and I found a passage that describes how incredible the brain is.

The teacher read: "One cubic centimeter of brain contains ten billion bits of information and it processes five thousand bits a second . . . the single most powerful statement to come out of brain research in the last twenty-five years is this . . . We are as different from one another on the inside of our heads as we appear to be different from one another on the outside of our heads."

TEACHER: In our last class, you examined how developed you felt in the use of your multiple intelligences. Maria has allowed us to use her response sheet. Notice her responses.

The teacher placed Maria's transparency on the overhead.

Developing Intelligences

	1 2 3 4 5 undeveloped highly developed		
Seven Intelligences	**What I know about myself**	**What I noticed today**	**Advice for next time**
Verbal/Linguistic	1 3+	*I liked working with a partner better. When we talked I noticed I had some good ideas. We came up with new ways to use the information. I wasn't as worried about reading when we could do it together.*	*not to worry. Talk a little more. to feel more relaxed. The talking today really worked for me.*
Logical/Mathematical	3 3+		
Visual/Spatial	4 4+		
Musical/Rhythmic	2 3		
Body/Kinesthetic	4 4		
Interpersonal	1 4+		
Intrapersonal	0 4		

TEACHER: Maria, can you talk to us about what you noticed about your use of your intelligences?

MARIA: I am a little embarrassed about how hard reading is for me. I felt much better because my partner and I worked together figuring out a way to show what we understood. I really knew what to do and I felt I had some really terrific ideas.

The authenticity of her response brought a stillness to the class.

TEACHER: Thank you, Maria. As we work today, I am going to ask you to again notice your thinking. Notice what works for you and how you might do things differently another time. In your triads, please number off one, two, three. Put your number and name on your paper and divide your page into three sections.

The students negotiated their numbers as the teacher drew an outline of a page, divided into three segments, on the board. Beside the model of the page the teacher drew:

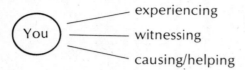

TEACHER: In the *Think-of-a-Time* strategy you will examine a key idea from three points of view. Our key idea is *conversations that work*. In the first space on your paper, jot down a time when you experienced a powerful conversation—one that flowed easily, one that you knew really worked.

Concepts of the curriculum are tied to personal experience.

The students pondered and then began to jot down experiences. The room stilled.

TEACHER: When you are ready, begin sharing your experiences in your triads. As you listen to your partners' experiences, think about why the conversations worked so well. You have five minutes.

The students began sharing their experiences. There was no management issue. They clearly enjoyed telling and learning each author's stories. The questions posed showed a climate of trust.

TEACHER: Five seconds . . . What was it that made the conversations so powerful?

STUDENTS: When both people were involved.

An interesting topic.

When you talk with someone that's been in the same situation.

TEACHER: Talk to us a little more about that.

Press for substantiation and elaboration of thought.

ELENA: Tammy and I were talking about a problem. She agreed with me a lot and she could feel my feelings because she once had the same problem with her brother.

TEACHER: Thank you. Students with number one on their papers, you will stand and move to another group. When you get there, compare with your new partners what it was that made successful conversations. You'll have one minute to share details.

Short-term interactions can help students to examine an issue from several points of view.

There was a murmur of conversation as accountability tightened. The students moved quickly into adjoining groups and immediately began talking. There was no time for resistance.

TEACHER: Five seconds . . . This time when you change roles, you will jot down a time when you witnessed someone having a powerful conversation. You were not included in the talk, but you knew it was working. You have three to four minutes to jot down ideas and five minutes to share your experiences.

They individually searched through their experiences then wrote. The talk reflected deep connections to the concept of conversation.

TEACHER: Five seconds . . . Let's listen to a few stories and notice what made them powerful. Don't put your hand up. I'll call on you. Jason.

JASON: The conversation was intense. There were hand motions and expressions on people's faces. It was emotional because one person was crying.

TEACHER: Thank you Jason.

BECKY: The person looked interested. They were both not looking around. I could see them taking turns and taking what one person did and building on it.

DAVID: The person seemed to get into the other person's space. Even though he didn't agree he said things like, ''I know you think that but have you considered . . .'' I noticed they kind of treated each other the same way. They even seemed to move their hands and heads in the same way.

Everyone laughed in recognition of similar experiences.

JENNIFER: Lots of eye contact and the person I saw reached out and put her arm around the other person. Lots of understanding.

TEACHER: You are building sophisticated details about effective conversations. These details will grow to be our criteria as we explore blocks in a later class. Let's move on. Number two people say 'goodbye' and move to a new group. On arrival, compare what you noticed while observing effective conversations. How could you tell the conversation was effective?

Within ten seconds everyone was settled and engaged.

TEACHER: Five seconds . . . This time you are to jot down a time when you helped or supported someone in a conversation. You might talk about that in your group before you begin to write.

As I walked around, I could hear students talk about supporting family members and friends. Rich interactions revealed life experiences to draw upon.

TEACHER: Five seconds . . . How did you support or help people in conversations? As you listen to the responses, notice what works because when you move into your last grouping, you will be making a list of critical attributes of effective conversations.

STUDENT: I helped someone break up. I had to be sensitive, caring, and quite strict.

TEACHER: Tell us what that looked like and sounded like.

STUDENT: Well, I had to help each of them hear each other. It was tense, but when I said things like, ''so you're feeling . . .'' the people would talk on.

The teacher acknowledged the response and elicited responses from more students. She moved to stand near each group. I could hear her pressing for minute details of effective communication.

TEACHER: Let's hear a few more.

STUDENTS: When my friend had to tell her Mom she was pregnant I had to help her get the courage to face her parents. We actually practiced what she would say. We tried to get into many ways to tell the problem. I really know her parents, so I could get into being them. I was really feeling pressure to help her because this was a big one.

I supported my little brother when he was telling my Mom how well he did in his soccer game. When I described his plays, his eyes just shone. I could see how important it was for someone to add to his explanation.

I saw something my brother did. My Mom caught him and I helped him add more details so she would understand the whole picture.

I helped my brother talk to our doctor about an operation he had to have. I tried to show how my brother was feeling. The tricky part was not talking for him. When he seemed stuck, I asked him a question. He then was able to talk to the doctor. It was hard.

The teacher is anticipating that this aspect may be more difficult. By talking through the perspective first, the learner makes deeper connections.

The students are led to synthesize their understanding.

Understanding the interest of others is developed when we explore a concept as a supporter.

TEACHER: You've explored the concept of effective communication in a conversation from three perspectives. When number three's move, your triad will create a list of critical or important factors that make effective conversations. Send one member of your group to get a felt pen and a piece of chart paper.

The students talked briefly. Each group began to list important factors. After about five minutes, the teacher invited the groups to pass their papers to the next group. She had put a number on each chart paper and the papers were rotated clockwise.

TEACHER: This is a brief look at the *Carousel* strategy we'll use next class. Your job is to read what the other group wrote, respond to what they wrote, and add new ideas. You'll have about two minutes before we pass the papers.

Extend the learning experience beyond the original small group.

The students looked at each item, confirmed their ideas, and jotted down responses. The teacher moved from group to group encouraging them to jot down details of their discussion. After a short time, she called "pass" and the students responded to a new paper.

Consolidating ideas collaboratively fuels individual thought.

TEACHER: Pass the papers back to their owners. Look at the responses. What did you notice?

STUDENTS: The ideas are sort of the same but they are said differently.

We know a lot about conversations.

We got really involved and we had a lot of information to share.

I noticed we work better in groups.

TEACHER: It's good to have the option isn't it? Next class, we'll develop summaries when we finish the *Carousel*. Your ticket out today is a three-part reflection. On the back of your individual papers, respond to the points I have put on the board.

1. What you learned about effective conversations
2. What you noticed about your own learning
3. A goal for next time

Riki

- both partners give good auguements and we both had views and shared them. I knew he understood me.

- they were both interested in what they were talking about. close together - space.

- helped someone breakup, had to be, sensitive and caring yet strict!

1. - Important blocks to listening are that you shouldn't judge people, interupt people or get into dreaming. It's very rude to dream while you're supposed to be listening and also rude to interupt someone. To judge someone is to stereotype which is to be racist and to be racist is to be ignorant.

2. - My own learning is that if I could set my mind on something I want I will achieve my goal and I may or may not remember what I learned. The next time I will be more active, and try not to be so shy about my ideas.

TEACHER: While you are writing, our visitors will be preparing their reflections for you to hear. You have five minutes. The class ended with the students and teachers offering their insights.

All learners in the class share their reflections.

STUDENTS:

• What I noticed about myself is that I got involved and actually had alot of information to share. Goal for next time - got thoughts on paper - more detail.

• I feel that I worked well and learned quite a bit over the last hour. I never realized the things that go through your head when talking to people. Now I realize that I am guilty of some of the listening blocks. I will try to notice when I do those things. One goal is to look at the speaker more.

• I will try to discuss more. I think that I might have learned something this class and I am looking forward to next class. One goal is to try to focus more. My thoughts judge and wander.

• I noticed that I work better in groups. I will try harder and build on what others say. Eye contact is necessary.

TEACHERS: I thought that at the beginning of the sequence the students were somewhat hesitant to speak. Once they became involved, it was almost impossible to get them to stop.

I have noticed that with all of these strategies there is a real accountability. The feedback is immediate and powerful because it comes from peers.

The Next Class

A piece of chart paper for group work was distributed to each group prior to starting the class. One side was blank. The other side had a piece of information taped to it.

TEACHER: At the end of last class we used a *Carousel* strategy to pool our ideas about powerful conversation. We are going to use that process again today, only in a different way. Before I adapt the strategy, write in your learning log what you recall about the *Carousel* strategy. Michelle and Robert, you were absent last class. Our focus for this sequence is communication and what creates and blocks effective communication. Think of a time when you had a very powerful conversation with someone. Try to identify what factors made it such a powerful experience. Jot down your ideas.

Writing individually develops personal meaning before developing collective understanding.

After about three minutes, the teacher reconstructed the steps of the Carousel *with the students. She pressed them to articulate the "why" behind each step. She then reconstructed the factors the students had generated for effective conversation.*

Understanding the purpose and the process deepens knowledge.

TEACHER: What do we know about effective communication in conversations?

Networked connections reinforce and extend understanding.

The teacher networked connections including the two absentees.

TEACHER: Today we will examine a number of blocks to listening and how these blocks affect communication. We will work together on the first block, then we'll move into a *Carousel* and each group will have a different block to respond to. Today I have five blocks to cover—one per group. I will read some information about the first block, "judging". When I finish, turn to your group and talk about what facts struck you the most. Offer any connections, personal experiences, or questions.

The teacher read the passage. The students listened, then talked. As they talked in their small groups, she moved around the room.

TEACHER: Five . . . Thank you. On the chart paper, with your felt pen, jot down any ideas, connections, personal experiences, or questions you have about judging. Everything important you talked about needs to go down on the paper. Use words, idea sketches— anything to show your connections.

As the students responded, the teacher continued moving among the groups. She then invited groups to share their responses, and to notice the unique ways each group chose to represent their understandings.

Modeling distributes understandings and validates multiple ways of responding to information.

STUDENTS: We thought judging blocks listening because the person gets stuck on stereotypes. Racists can't get past their blocks because they judge the person by the outside instead of the inside. They hear the person but they don't listen. We think that's ignorant. People should push the block to the side and focus on the speaker.

I noticed that I judge people and I like to be right. Next time I will try to be more aware of what I'm doing.

We'll use only the felt pen to jot down all of our ideas. At first we all wanted to write down our own ideas. By talking them out first and having a recorder, we got the ideas clearer.

TEACHER: Yes. It is sometimes necessary to assume different roles in an effective group. Now work on the back of your chart paper. I am going to give each group information to read and to respond to on a *different* block to listening. You can talk and jot down ideas directly on the chart paper then you will pass your papers, just like last class, and respond to the whole page—the listening block and the responses of the previous group. We will pass five times, then you will get your paper back to summarize and present. Your personal ticket out the door at the end of this class will be to document:

- what you know about blocks to listening;
- what you noticed about your learning;
- a learning goal for next time.

This time, the groups had to read the text on their own. Some groups read it silently, others chose a spokesperson to read to them. A few students were challenged by the level of the reading, but they worked together and talked it through. The students wrote all over the large pages—underlining words, drawing arrows, and sketching pictures that related to the blocks to listening. After five passes, everyone looked tired. The papers were returned to the original groups and the teacher gave them ten minutes to develop a summary and a way to present their findings. Some sketched, while others created role-play situations, TV interviews, and written explanations.

Each group made their presentation. The teacher invited the students to listen to the presentations and note the content and the effectiveness of the form. The class ended with the three-part reflections.

The Next Class

A second six blocks to listening was examined using the *Carousel* process. Students set individual goals for themselves as listeners, based on the twelve blocks of listening they had examined.

Cross-Curricular Applications

Think-of-a-Time

1. *Social Studies*

    In a study of World War II and its impact on life in Canada, students were about to research Japanese internment camps. To focus this study from the point of view of the Japanese, students were asked to think about the following situations.

    1. Think of a time when you were penalized or unjustly treated and you didn't understand why.
    2. Think of a time when you watched someone being unjustly treated and you didn't understand why.
    3. Think of a time when you were part of a group who treated another person or group unjustly, without understanding why you were doing this.

2. *English*

    While studying *To Kill A Mockingbird* by Harper Lee, students examined the character of Atticus using this sequence.

    1. Think of a time when you stood up for what you believed in, even though you had to go against the opinion of the majority.
    2. Think of a time when you witnessed someone going against the crowd to defend what she or he believed in.
    3. Think of a time when you supported someone who held an unpopular opinion.

Carousel

1. *Social Studies*

    Grade eleven students studying the Great Depression were invited to study sets of pictures set up at different places in the room. In small groups, they were to identify key ideas and develop a set of questions.

What are the characteristics of an economy in depression?
Why would they be on strike during depression?
How could they go ballroom dancing when the community around them is suffering from the effects of the depression?
Where did they get money?
How can people keep all their money when everyone else is starving?
What was the chance of the children surviving?
Was there alot of pollution?
Why did families have so many children with so little money?

2. *English*

   Illustrations, in sequence, from "The Highwayman" by Alfred Noyes were set up around the room. Pairs of students walked through the sequence twice—the first time walking quickly and starting at the first picture, and the second time, starting randomly, and moving slowly from picture to picture. Their task was to decide what they thought the story was about. The class ended with an individual writing session.

3. *Mathematics*

   The teacher placed a different word problem on each of six chart papers. In a small group, students solved the problems and listed how they reached the solution. The papers passed to new groups. The groups analyzed the steps and responded with advice and questions. After three rotations, the papers were returned to their original owners. The groups designed ways to teach others how to solve their problems. The class ended with the students solving two problems independently and reflecting on their learning.

Powerful

Solve these problems and explain your thinking

1. F x D = W

500 n x 4 Km = 2000 KJ

W
2000 ÷ 500 = 4

FxD = W
Divided work by force, got distance
2000 ÷ 500 = 4 km

F x D = W
500 n x ___ = 2000 KJ
2000 ÷ 500 = 4

He can travel (4 Km)

2. force is 500 N. Times it by # 5 km. Need 2500 Jules of energy work. He will do 2500 Jules of work

Energy and work are the same thing.

Reflection...
1. What I noticed about my learning over the past three afternoons....
   I noticed that I learn better with hands on experiments

2. How could you make your learning more powerful next time? I could eat more for lunch and explain or help others.

4. *Physical Education*

   The teacher showed a segment of a video skill sequence. Students pooled their understandings on a chart paper and responded to one another's questions before viewing further sections. The teacher then put the class in a similar sequence to apply the understandings. Students reflected on their skill acquisition until the end of the class.

THINK-OF-A-TIME 1-2-3

1. Students are grouped in threes and numbered one, two, three.

2. Students examine a concept or an issue from three points of view:
   - as a participant;
   - as a witness;
   - as a casual agent or a supporter.

3. Students respond individually in writing, compare their stories with their triad members, and collect common attributes of these stories.

4. After exploring each point of view, one student from each triad joins a new group: first one's move, then two's, then three's.

5. This last triad develops a set of attributes or elements critical to the concept being examined.

6. A class list of attributes is generated.

7. Individuals reflect on what they now know about the concept, what they noticed about themselves as learners, and identify one goal for the next time they engage in the process.

CAROUSEL

1. Students are grouped for collaborative work. The data to be examined (print information, pictures, or artifacts) corresponds to the number of student groups in the class.

2. Each group responds to their data on a response paper that stays with the data.

3. After five to ten minutes, student groups move to a new data set or the data set moves to them. Students read, discuss, and respond by adding new information, answering questions, and asking further questions.

4. Student groups move through the sets of data.

5. Students work together to develop a summary of the classes' responses to their piece of the data. Groups present their findings and work collectively to develop criteria for powerful demonstrations of understanding.

6. Each student shows his or her understanding, reflects on his or her learning, and gives himself or herself advice for next time.

6

Anticipation Guide

Verification of assertions and hypotheses is fundamental to scientific inquiry and philosophy . . . students need to grow in their awareness of the richness of methods and procedures for confirming or disconfirming something, in understanding that the nature of the claim, and in their thoroughness in requiring firm evidence . . .

— R. J. Marzanno et al, *Dimensions of Thinking*

. . . mastering the skills necessary to realize that intelligence, and collaborating with others — are prerequisites for creativity in adult life. Perhaps nowhere is this more critical than in the work we do.

— D. Coleman, P. Kaufman & M. Ray, *The Art of Creativity*

Misconceptions about a topic are not likely to be discarded entirely unless conflicting information from a content area text is actively confronted.

— F. Duffelmeyer & D. Baum, *The Extended Anticipation Guide Revisited*

Most areas of study that are at all worth our attention entail far more complexity than is acknowledged in . . . curriculum . . . people's intellectual engagement, when they are given the chance to pursue these complexities according to their own lights, is extraordinary.

— E. Duckworth, *Twenty-four, Forty-two, and I Love You: Keeping it Complex*

The grade eleven students had been immersed in global issues surrounding endangered species.

TEACHER: Today you will be using an *Anticipation Guide* to set up some new connections in preparation for studying an article from an issue of *The Globe and Mail*. We'll look at five statements, one at a time. You will decide whether you agree or disagree with each statement. Give support for your position. You will compare your ideas, then work with a partner to develop what you think the essence of the article will be. We will see and/or hear several responses to consider what is working. Then you and your partner will present your response to one other group and receive feedback. We will end the class with reflection on what you noticed about your thinking throughout the process. For homework, you'll read the article.

Students need to access prior knowledge and be prepared to have this challenged if new connections are to be made.

Students focused as the teacher listed the day's action plan on the board.

Learning requires personal commitment.

The teacher revealed the first item on the Anticipation Guide *and invited the students to answer "yes" or "no" to the statement and provide written evidence or support for their position. She gave them a few minutes to generate a response before signalling a five-second time for moving on.*

Substantiating deepens connections to content focus.

Effort Plan		**ANTICIPATION GUIDE**	*Name*
			Block
			Date

Answer Yes or No. Support your response.

	You	**Writer**
1. 80% of Quebecers live along the St. Lawrence.		
2. Approximately 1 in 5 Canadians (ie. 5 million people get their drinking water from the St. Lawrence River.		
3. The St. Lawrence beluga is the most polluted mammal on earth.		
4. The majority of St. Lawrence belugas have died because of the failure of their immune system.		
5. If the belugas die, we could die.		

Reflection:

TEACHER: Turn to your partner and share your positions. Remember, you can change your mind from your original position if your partner is particularly convincing.

Everyone in the room talked. Some had substantial reasoning, some were quite superficial. The students listened respectfully to one another—evidence that this was not a new process for them. Some students changed their responses after talking with a partner.

TEACHER: Five seconds . . .

TEACHER: I'm going to go through each of the remaining four items, stopping for two minutes for you to respond, and then I'll give you two minutes to talk. At the end of the fifth statement, we'll create a class tally of your perspectives and hear one another's theories.

The process unfolded very smoothly. After each item, the students pondered, responded, and talked through their understandings.

TEACHER: Five seconds . . .

The teacher read item number one, "80% of Quebecers live along the St. Lawrence," and counted the "yes" or "no" position. She wrote "22 yes" and "8 no" on the overhead transparency.

TEACHER: If you said "yes", please give us your reasons.

STUDENTS: I think the river is key to farming and to the industries. I read somewhere that the parcels of land are long and narrow so many people backed onto the river.

Most large cities are located on or along transportation routes and I think most people live in urban areas.

TEACHER: What about someone who can describe their thinking for the "no" position?

STUDENT: I think that 80% is too high for just along one river in a place as big as Quebec. There must be other rivers for people to live along.

The teacher resisted giving her own opinion to any of the responses. Each of the five items was reread, the number of "yes" and "no" responses tallied, and explanation of the thinking behind both "yes" and "no" responses heard.

Deepen individual connections by defending one's position with a partner.

This signal offers students the opportunity to complete discussion naturally, respecting that conversations need time for completion.

Establishing the structure hastens the process.

Opportunities for data analysis are integrated into the study.

Shared understandings deepen connection to concepts.

Effort Plan		ANTICIPATION GUIDE

Name

Block

Date

Answer Yes or No. Support your response.

	You		Writer
	Yes	No	
1. 80% of Quebecers live along the St. Lawrence.	22	8	
2. Approximately 1 in 5 Canadians (ie. 5 million) people get their drinking water from the St. Lawrence River.	10	20	
3. The St. Lawrence beluga is the most polluted mammal on earth.	15	15	
4. The majority of St. Lawrence belugas have died because of the failure of their immune system.	10	20	
5. If the belugas die, we could die.	24	6	

Reflection:

TEACHER: Now you have heard positions on five key ideas from an article that we'll be rereading. Your job is to work with your partner to develop what you think will unfold in an article that holds these ideas. You can present your ideas in any form you choose. What questions would you like to ask before we begin?

STUDENT: Do we have to write?

TEACHER: No. What other forms could you use?

STUDENT: A drawing.

TEACHER: Absolutely. What else?

Students need to work with their conceptions and misconceptions if new information is to be actively considered.

Value multiple ways of demonstrating understandings

STUDENTS: a TV interview

a political cartoon

a trial

a press release

an ad campaign

TEACHER: You choose. You have about ten minutes to generate a collaborative response. Then we will listen to a number of drafts to hear what's working in your writing and to use this as a foundation for criteria for powerful presentations.

The students quickly began talking about content and about form. They explored many ways of connecting ideas. They often referred to the statements on their Anticipation Guides *and to the tally of responses on the overhead.*

TEACHER: You have worked hard from only kernels of information. You analyzed, interpreted, and evaluated key concepts, then you created unique responses. We'll hear a few and decide on what criteria we want to consider when presenting this response.

The teacher had placed a different-numbered card beside each pair of students. Instead of asking for volunteers to present, she called out a number. The students were very comfortable presenting response drafts and spoke with ease. The community of learners listened intently and clapped enthusiastically before offering evidence of power.

TEACHER: What caught your attention? What worked? What was powerful?

After listening to four presentations, the students had noticed that powerful anticipations and theories share certain characteristics.

The instruction includes complex, authentic tasks.

Assessment is in context.

Accountability is designed to build criteria through student responses. Self-assessment is integrally tied to both content and process.

Value the rigorous cognitive engagement.

Student level of engagement heightens when it is expected that all will respond.

**Powerful Anticipations and
Powerful Theories are. . .**

- believable
- consistent with data
- original, sometimes humorous
- compare/contrast ideas of both partners
- confirm ideas you think are true

The students then moved into heterogenous groups of four—those with even numbered cards joined with a pair with an odd number.

Varying the grouping builds flexibility and adaptability.

TEACHER: With your partner, listen to the other pair present their theory and give feedback. Try to have your feedback directly tied to the criteria we developed. Decide if this criteria needs revision.

I listened in on an interaction . . .

STUDENT PAIR #1: We think this article is going to be about how industry along the river is polluting the belugas and everything because we are trying to be economical so that our prices are competitive. That's why we have the car and the Coke coming out of the end of the process.

STUDENT PAIR #2 That's neat! I like the way your drawing makes a line just like an assembly line. That's a good image. If you are going to be "consistent with data" like the criteria say, do you think you should be saying something about whether or not Canadians are drinking this water from the St. Lawrence?

STUDENT PAIR #1: You can assume that people would be because the factory is built on the river.

STUDENT PAIR #2: Maybe. But just if the people looking at your illustration think the same way you do. Did you guys think that one in five Quebeckers really get their drinking water from the St. Lawrence? Don't you think that ratio is inflated?

I was intrigued by the weaving together of personal belief and reference to the information generated and presented in class. The tone of the conversation was respectful.

TEACHER: Do you have anything to add to or remove from our list?

A few students raised their hands. Some changes were added.

STUDENT: I think we should take off ''original, sometimes humorous''. Ours was a good theory and it wasn't either of those. That only happens sometimes.

TEACHER: Any disagreement? Is this always appropriate as criteria? . . . Then it is gone. Any other changes?

Assessment is ongoing and involves the students.

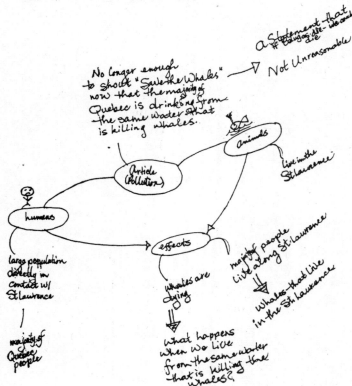

**Powerful Anticipations and
Powerful Theories are. . .**
(Continued)

- ideas developed with lots of support
- up-to-date and connects other things we know

TEACHER: You've heard a number of anticipations and noticed what made them effective. I'd like you to use the framework on the board to reflect on your learning today. The teacher had placed the reflection points on the board as they worked on their presentations.

Reflections

1. Key ideas
2. What you noticed about your learning
3. How you contributed to your partnership

The students are developing skills on reflecting on both content and process knowledge.

The students wrote fluently and with ease in expressing their understandings.

STUDENT SAMPLE:

> Through the process of creating a model of what we thought was going to be the major content of the article, I found that a different set of concepts, ideas and thoughts came to the top of our conversation. A model of the problem concerning humans was helpful in generating ideas of issues surrounding pollution. This process helped me move away from one line of thinking. I was able to see another perspective.

TEACHER: For homework, I want you to read the article. As you read, be prepared to be surprised by the author. Notice when he agrees with your response to the anticipation statements and when he challenges your views by disagreeing with your opinion. Is his evidence convincing enough to cause you to change your mind?
 Before you leave, I'd like to read the reflection that I wrote.

Students are explicitly encouraged to connect their work in personal and collaborative response to the information presented in the article.

I am noticing so much more accountability in these students, both in the class and in their homework. At the beginning of the year, they moaned when I even mentioned homework. Now, I keep it clearly linked to concepts key to our study and I make it open-ended. The criteria developed with the students have opened up incredible applications. We're all delighted with the original, effective applications. All students are offered opportunities to succeed in their own way.

The teacher as a learner is constantly modeled.

The students smiled and moved to their next class.

61

The Next Class

The students worked in their teams of four to consider the writer's response to each of the *Anticipation Guide* statements. They individually webbed in response to "What I Know Now", then generated individual research questions based on "What I Want to Find Out".

By Andre Picard

The Globe and Mail
TADOUSSAC, Que.

The whistled song of the beluga, the white whale they call the canary of the sea, is an unforgettable, heartwrenching dirge. It ripples across the surface of the chilly St. Lawrence, caresses the fjords of the Saguenay, and echoes around the world—a tremulous, child-like cry for help.

The song that too few have heard accompanied by the rhythm of the waves is not only a lament for a species on the brink of extinction but also a brutal reminder of the enormity of the human assault on the precious natural resource that is the St. Lawrence River.

Five million Quebeckers depend on the St. Lawrence for their drinking water. Eighty per cent of the province's 6.5 million residents, and much of the wildlife, live along the river's 4,500-kilometre shore line. The river is the economic and ecological heart of the province. The 400 remaining belugas— their ancestors slaughtered for sport, their food supply poisoned by chemicals and heavy metals, their beautiful white skin deformed by grotesque cancers, and their reproductive abilities threatened by genetic mutations—have become a symbol. Like the canary released in a coal mine to test the air, the canary of the seas test the troubled waters.

The message is simple," says Pierre Beland, scientific director of the St. Lawrence National Centre for Ecotoxicology in Rimouski, Que. "If the belugas die, we could die."

Cross-Curricular Applications

1. *Physical Education*

   After an Olympic win by Kerrin Lee-Gartner, students used an *Anticipation Guide* to speculate on critical forces contributing to her success. An article featuring Kerrin was processed using the *Four Quadrants of Thought*.

Effort Plan		

ANTICIPATION GUIDE

Name _____

Block _____

Date _____

Answer Yes or No. Support your response.

	Before	After
1. Talent in an Olympic athlete determines success.	yes, because if you don't have talent you don't get anywhere	
2. Serious injury signals the end of Olympic hopes.	No, you can work your way back to help if you want to	
3. The right ski's make a difference.	You bet! Talent and equipment are a team.	
4. Aggressiveness is the most important quality in an Olympic skier.	Yes. Courage and will to win. Go for it attitude.	

Reflection:

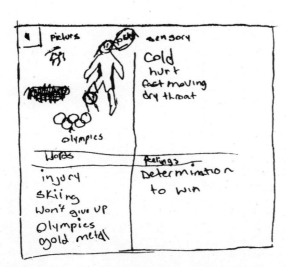

63

2. *Learning for Living*
   Students developed, presented, and evaluated hypotheses related to work, energy, and energy requirements. Their demonstrations included sports interviews, press releases, diagrams, and drawings.

Effort Plan		ANTICIPATION GUIDE

Name

Block

Date

Answer Yes or No. Support your response.

	You	Writer
Surplus energy is stored as body fat ready to be used when needed.		
Boys requires more kilojoules of energy per day than girls.		
A hamburger and bun has more kilojoules of energy than four oatmeal cookies.		
Collin is running a race that requires 300 kj/m. He has eaten a hot dog and a bun. Can he run for ten minutes.		
Considering your food intake, do you have enough energy to operate as a lab scientist for the rest of the afternoon.		

Reflection:

64

3. *English*

Students completed an *Anticipation Guide*, then collaboratively constructed a story, prior to reading "The Dinner Party" by Mona Gardner.

Effort Plan		ANTICIPATION GUIDE	Name
			Block
			Date

Answer Yes or No. Support your response.

	You	Writer
1. Women have outgrown the jumping-on-a-chair-at-the-sight-of-a-mouse era.		
2. Cobras always attack when close to people.		
3. Women tend not to show more calm and cool behavior in tense situations than men.		
4. Cobras follow trails of milk.		
5. Government dinner parties in India are usually served by servants.		

Reflection:

4. *Social Studies*

Before processing an article on the rainforest, the students generated, presented, and assessed predictions. Following the study of the article, the teacher invited them to show their understandings in a *Concept Map*.

Effort	Plan	ANTICIPATION GUIDE	Name
		The Vanishing Rainforest	Block
			Date

Answer Yes or No. Support your response.

	You	Author
Brazil has few energy reserves and needs large amounts of hydro-electricity for power.		
1/3 of all the worlds rainforest are found in Brazil.		
The forest land in Brazil is very rich and good for growing crops.		
The rainforest is a source of such things as rubber and cancer-fighting drugs.		
Money to pay for building new dams comes from countries like Canada.		

Reflection:

ANTICIPATION GUIDE

1. Identify major concepts in a text selection, video, or demonstration.

2. Turn the concepts into four or five statements and develop a response form.

3. Group students in pairs.

4. Invite students to respond to statements one at a time, stopping after each response to have them talk through their opinions.

5. Develop a class tally for each statement and discuss opinions while pressing for elaboration and substantiation.

6. Invite partners to collaboratively generate an anticipation.

7. Listen to draft anticipations and notice what works.

8. Regroup students into groups of four for peer presentations and feedback.

9. Refine developing criteria.

10. Students reflect individually.

11. Students read the article or view the new information.

12. Students compare their original responses to the *Anticipation Guide* statements with possible responses of the author.

7

From Gallery Walk to Collaborative Summaries

. . . discipline of team learning involves mastering the practices of dialogue and discussion . . . In dialogue, there is free and creative exploration of complex, subtle issues, a deep 'listening' to one another . . . in discussion different views are presented and defended and there is a search for the best view to support decisions.

— P.M. Senge, *The Fifth Discipline*

Working together to get the job done increases students' abilities to provide leadership, build and maintain trust, communicate effectively, and manage conflicts constructively. Employability and career success depend largely on such social skills.

— D.W. Johnson & R.T. Johnson, *Classroom Instruction and Cooperative Learning*

If they gain skills in observing what they and others do, in analyzing what happens and why, in taking the risk of trialling new behaviours and observing the results, they then have gained the power to decide what happens in their lives.

— J. McFadden, C. Flynn & B. Bazzo, *Life Science: Making Your Life a Success*

. . . criteria, when used in appraising samples of student writing, suggest where to focus efforts to improve . . . criteria . . . should be used to guide the continuing improvement of the student's effectiveness in writing for the various purposes in which writing could be used in his or her situation.

— R.W. Tyler, *General Statement on Program Evaluation*

Prior to the class, the teacher had set up eight focus areas in the art room, each one featuring important aspects of Monet's style. The grade nine students were beginning a study of Impressionist artists. The teacher had a graph outlining the learning sequence on the chalkboard.

Set the stage for a sequence.

Connecting	Processing	Personalizing/Transforming
Gallery Walk • Eight aspects of Monet's style	• **Collaborative Summaries**	

TEACHER: To bring you into Monet's style, we will begin the class with a *Gallery Walk*. This is an adaptation of the *Carousel* strategy. You and your table partner will visit each of the eight areas set up in the room. You will study the material, talk, and record important aspects of Monet's style. I am really interested in how you and your partner collaborate so, in five minutes, I will stop you and ask you to tell us how the talk is helping your understanding. After twenty minutes, your job will be to identify the six most important elements in his style. We'll then begin a negotiation process called a *Collaborative Summary*.

Extend and apply prior process knowledge.

A purpose is set for the partner interaction.

Response sheets with the eight area headings listed were distributed to each student. The students moved into the Gallery Walk *and the teacher moved around the room. After five minutes, she signalled with a flick of the lights.*

The teacher orchestrates the experience then interacts, supporting and extending the learning.

TEACHER: How is your interaction with your partner helping you to understand the material?

ELIZABETH: When Crystal says something, I get other ideas. We have to keep thinking about his style because there's lots of interesting things that really aren't important to his life.

TEACHER: Thank you. Keep noticing important aspects of his style. You have about fifteen minutes to visit the areas. I'll remind you when there are five minutes left so you can gauge your timing.

Modeling how partners support each other's learning deepens interaction skills.

Five minutes before moving into the next process, the teacher flicked the lights. Most students were near completion. To bring this process to a close, the teacher suggested they might want to finish their walk with a quick stop by each area to confirm connections and to add any possible new connections.

THE GALLERY WALK

MONET

STEAM ENGINE

- moist concrete definition-
  movement known as impression
- concentrated on the
  movement

ROUEN CATHEDRAL

- detailed
- painted how he felt not
  what it looked like
- used certain colors to
  determine the time of day
- caught light on structure at different
  times of day

WATERLILIES

- most difficult because
  always changed
- bright/dull colors
- emphasizes lines, shape,
  color

CARTOONS

detailed
exaggerated characteristics
colors - moods?

EARLY PAINTINGS

- loading a pistol with paint
  & firing it at a dry canvas

LIGHT

- emphasized light & color
- used color to express
  feelings about nature

ART CRITIC

- face shows moods
- disturbing objects
  in characters

THE POPLARS

- didn't think nature
  could be captured in
  one image
- worked on as many
  as 10 canvases a day
- drew picture over
  as light changed.

TEACHER: When you are finished, look over your sheet with your partner. Think about the most important aspects of his style. In five minutes you will turn your individual papers over and make a personal list.

The students were focused. Those who were finished went back to their tables and began discussing their findings.

TEACHER: What have you noticed about your thinking so far today?

KEVIN: I thought this was going to be boring, but once I got into it I found it quite interesting.

JOHN: When I work with others, they get ideas and it makes me click in and get lots of ideas. I wouldn't be able to do it without help.

JACKIE: I worked fast because I also thought it was interesting.

HEIDI: I realized more about Monet. Everything worked for me.

TEACHER: Thank you. You've had a brief immersion in Monet's style. Put a 1-5 scale on the top of the opposite side of your page. As we move into the next process, notice the amount of effort you invest in your learning. We'll be reflecting on that effort at the end of the class.

Externalizing reflections values diverse engagement with the learning.

Commitment to learning is continually deepened by having the students monitor their own involvement.

Individually, decide and list your six most important items. When you finish your list, move to find another person who has finished and negotiate a shared list. You need to create one list of six items that you both agree on.

Interest was sparked again. Friends made eye contact. They obviously were keen to choose their partners.

TEACHER: When you and your partner reach agreement on six items, jot them down on your paper. Together, find another pair to negotiate with. Once again, negotiate until you reach agreement. Your task as a team of four will be to compose a summary of Monet's style that you might find in an art gallery catalog. We will listen to summaries to develop criteria before you write your own summary. We will only stop once to notice what is working in your negotiations. Begin your list now.

The teacher outlined the steps on the board as individuals began writing.

---

1. List six important aspects
2. Negotiate with a partner
3. Negotiate in groups of four
4. Compose a team summary
5. Present summaries and build criteria
6. Reflect
7. Prepare own summary

Very soon, individuals found partners. The negotiations were alive with evidence of understanding. Some individuals returned to the Gallery Walk areas to support their positions. The teacher stopped the group once most people were in partners.

TEACHER: You have been negotiating for a few minutes now. How many of you feel you are accomplishing the task?

The response was positive.

TEACHER: Let's hear about your ways of reaching consensus.

Students raised their hands and the teacher pointed to volunteers.

ELIZABETH: We looked through our lists to see if we had any the same.

DAVID: We listened and joined ideas that were the same.

BECKY: We tossed ideas back and forth, listening a lot before we agreed.

A number of approaches were shared. In about ten minutes a list of criteria for successful negotiation was generated:

- be willing to reach agreement
- listen and build on each other's ideas
- be open to new ideas
- be willing to re-think ideas and wording
- show respect for each other's ideas
- have a sense of humor

Making explicit ways of reaching agreement expands learners' options.

TEACHER: That was quite a chunk of time! Before you begin negotiating again, notice if there is any part of the criteria that would be especially helpful as the focus of your negotiation, then continue negotiating. When you reach consensus in your group of four, begin your catalog summary.

Revision of approaches makes assessment a moment of learning.

Students worked with their partners and then in groups of four. The process was smooth and consensus was reached much more quickly than expected. Teams of four poured over their summary, carving out collective meaning. The teacher stopped them ten minutes before the bell.

TEACHER: You have worked very hard today. These summaries are to be included in a gallery catalog. Let's listen to one and see what really works.

Audience, purpose, and form are aligned.

Monet liked to swirl and blend while he mixed contrasting colors. He emphasized lines, shape and color to express his feelings towards nature. He wanted to paint what he felt life and not how it looked so he did 3 or 4 paintings because the mood changed

1 2 3 4 5

effort today

I learned more by walking around and having to share what I thought with other people.

TEACHER: What struck you? What held your attention?

KEVIN: The images and the flow of the words. I could feel motion.

JESSE: I could see the paintings we visited in the walk by hearing the words.

SHEILA: Life-like.

KELLY: Not too many words.

TEACHER: I'd like you each to present to another team. Move into groups of eight and, as you listen to the summary, notice what made it powerful.

The students returned to their tables to reflect.

TEACHER: Look back at your effort scale. Circle the amount of effort you maintained through this new process.

You created your own list. You negotiated in pairs, then in groups of four before working in a team to compose a summary. Before you leave today, list what you now know about Monet's style, and write one reflection on your own learning. For next class, prepare your own summary. You will be presenting it to the team you worked with today and they will give you feedback.

0 1 2 3 4 5
effort

(individual list)
First draft

1. Paintings were realistic.
2. He had a style all his own.
3. He painted 10 pictures a day!
4. He always had blue in his pictures.
5. Did a lot of outdoor pictures.
6. Did different brushstrokes

(negotiated list)
second draft

1. Painted 10 pictures a day.
2. Used dull colors + his paintings are realistic.
3. Used various different brush strokes.
4. Wanted to capture the impression.
5. He had a style all his own.
6. Did a lot of outdoor pictures.

(negotiated list)
third list

1. Paintings were realistic.
2. He painted from a bird's eye view.
3. He used fler + colors.
4. He used various different brush strokes.
5. Painted 10 pix a day with vibrant colors
6. Wanted to catch the impression.

Paintings were realistic + usually painted from a birds eye view. He used vibrant colors and did a lot of outdoor paintings. In each painting you could see the various brushstrokes. He seemed to have a style all his own.

- did outdoor paintings.
- really showed the various brushstrokes
- realistic paintings.
- He had a style all his own.
- He used fler + colors.
- He painted 10 pix a day!

I think my effort was
5/5!

I think I accomplished ALOT more than usual today.

The growth of content knowledge through the three negotiations was substantial. The students seemed genuinely surprised by how much their learning had deepened and how engaged they had become. The challenging learners were on-task and their documentation reflected growth.

1. concentrated on shapes and objects instead of subject matter.
2. cartoons mostly of important people
3. brush strokes were different everytime
4. He used all colors bright and dull — mixed them and used shadow
5. He was the first modern artist.
6. He painted over time and from different perspectives

4⁺ easier in a group and easier if you help people

What I noticed today -	Advice for next time
I'm not good with words.	CONCENTRATE on what you're doing!!!
I came across more ideas	
lots of design ideas,	
• accomplished lots and learned it better doing it	When I work with others they get ideas + it we click in + get lots of ideas!
• worked quite well in groups	
• wouldn't be able to do without help!	effort - 5⁺

+5 I have a lot of knowledge of Claude Monet.

The Next Class

As the students entered the room, the teacher invited them to walk through the eight areas to refresh their understanding of Monet. Students were called upon to present individual drafts. Criteria were refined for powerful summaries before students presented in teams of four, offering one another feedback and assessing themselves using familiar categories.

Cross-Curricular Applications

1. *Geometry*
   Individuals generated real-life applications for geometry in pairs, then in groups of four. As a group, the class compiled a list of reasons for studying geometry.

2. *Physical Education*
   One person generated dance steps to a piece of music. Pairs and squares collaborated to create a dance sequence to be performed. Individuals created and assessed their own dance sequence, based on the elements studied.

3. *English*
   Individuals generated evidence of a character's development from individual novels they were reading. Students, in pairs and then in groups of four, discussed and compared their characters. A Venn diagram was used to compare characters. Individuals designed a way to encourage reading of their novel by introducing a character.

4. *Safety in the Woodworking Lab*
   Individuals designed key elements of a safe workshop. Students, in pairs and then in groups of four, collaboratively generated a safe environment before comparing their elements with government safety regulations. Individuals created ways to teach lab safety standards to a small group.

5. *Mathematics*
   When solving estimation problems, students came to consensus on the best estimate. They then used their reasoning and evidence to convince others that *their* estimate was most reasonable.

COLLABORATIVE SUMMARIES

1. Individuals represent important aspects of a study (3-6).

2. Pairs negotiate to reach a consensus. Criteria for effective negotiation are developed after the students engage in the process.

3. Students can use the criteria to assess and alter their approaches to negotiating.

4. Students, in pairs and then in groups of four, continue negotiating. A collaborative summary is generated.

5. Criteria for powerful summaries are developed through student collaborative samples.

6. Teams present to one another using the criteria as a filter for feedback.

7. Individuals reflect on content understandings and on their learning.

8. Individuals write their own summaries.

8

Listen—Sketch—Draft

It may be that thoughtful literacy cannot be fully mobilized without a strong sense of community — without widening circles of meaning, through which individuals can understand themselves and their condition and construct coherent, purposeful lives.

— R. Brown, *Schools of Thought*

When students have opportunities to review their learning, especially with peers, they develop a wider range of skills and begin assuming more responsibility in shaping their own educational experiences.

— N. White, T. Blythe & H. Gardner, *Multiple Intelligences Theory: Creating the Thoughtful Classroom*

Students are challenged to . . . produce many works . . . exploring many aspects . . . judge their own work, as it is in progress . . . collaborate . . . a critical element of working and thinking as active learners . . . discussing, sharing, learning from others' perceptions . . .

— D.N. Perkins, *Educating for Insight*

Popularizers of brain research, like Buzan (1974), believe that representing situations with pictures as well as words activates the visual and verbal parts of the brain. It is suggested that this enhances access to knowledge by creating linkages to more parts of the brain.

— J.A. Minstrell, *Teaching Science for Understanding*

TEACHER: Today's story from the Asian Pacific Rim is called "A Ge-ware Incense Burner". In order to set the stage for this story, I am going to read several phrases to you from the text. I will read these phrases twice. Once you have heard them, I want you to choose a way of responding. Your choices are:

- to write three predictions about the short story;
- to write three questions you wonder about;
- to draw three sketches representing what is on your mind.

Encourage multiple ways of responding.

Before I read these phrases, I am interested in how well you know yourselves. Which of the forms of responding do you anticipate you will use? Jot it down on your paper.

The grade eleven English class had quickly been focused. As they noted their preferred response form, several students murmured to one another about which representation they would never do, and about how well they understood their various ways of understanding. As an observer, I was intrigued by the teacher's first focus being on the thinking/learning process. I had anticipated that she would spend more time establishing the different context for the short story.

TEACHER: These are the phrases. Remember that I will read them twice so you can begin by listening. Respond whenever you are ready.

A Ge-ware incense burner . . .
. . . myths . . . are fairly common . . .
. . . proprietors spread such tantalizing rumors . . .
. . . the idea . . . has an almost irresistible appeal . . .
. . . displayed in a glass cabinet . . .
. . . using for the purpose a bamboo ear spoon . . .
. . . stands in Antiques Alley operate on a self-service basis . . .
. . . the three of them came once again . . .

Everyone was listening, many with puzzled expressions on their faces. The teacher read slowly, giving the students time to question, to connect and re-connect, and then began to read again.

TEACHER: Alright. Take a few moments and respond to the phrases. Please work individually. We will hear or see some of your choices in a few minutes.

Individual voice is heard in making meaning . . . all are expected to respond.

Some of the students were already bent over their papers. Others searched the ceiling for possibilities, then responded. As we moved among them, I could see that many had asked questions, although most had predicted that they would generate predictions. Several of the students had sketched.

TEACHER: Did anything surprise you about your response?

DAVE: I always predict. But those phrases were *so* weird I had to ask questions.

Students are encouraged to change their strategy to fit the context.

TEACHER: Can you give us examples of your questions?

DAVE: Sure. What's an ear spoon?

They all laughed. It was clearly a question that was on most minds. Sure enough, however, another student had drawn her version of an ear spoon.

NUZHAT: I wondered what was gay-wear?

TEACHER: Does your thinking or question change if I show you the word *ge-ware*?

There was laughter again, as she nudged them into considering life beyond immediate, flash responses.

CLAUDIA: And I want to know who's coming again. Those three they talked about?

TEACHER: Anyone want to show us their sketches or tell us their predictions?

She wove together several more student responses, then continued.

TEACHER: You know how I prize questions. As I start to help you answer some of your questions, and hopefully generate new questions, I want you to reserve part of your thinking to notice when you are surprised and, if you can, how this surprise happens.

The strategy we are using today to process this story is called *Listen—Sketch—Draft*. To work with this strategy, you need to divide your paper into four boxes. I will read the first part of the story to you, and as I read, I invite you to sketch what comes to your mind while I am reading. Notice the timing. You sketch *as* I read. Notice also, that this is *not* a drawing competition. I am interested in the visual representations you make while you are listening. You can't be wrong. These sketches represent your thinking.

Let's see, by a show of hands, how many of you feel quite developed in this way of thinking. You think this will be quite easy. How many of you think this will be challenging? Take a moment and tell someone close to you how this part of the strategy makes you feel.

The students burst into conversation. There was a split of opinion on whether or not this was a reasonable expectation, and if this would support listening. I, too, was leery.

TEACHER: The second step in the strategy is conversation. Judging by the last couple of minutes, this may be a more developed way of seeking understanding for many of you. After you have sketched and I have stopped reading, you will have a few moments to talk with a partner about what you were doing on your paper and what you were thinking about. Then we will collect several key concepts from that part of the text. You will talk briefly to decide on what you want to remember from the text, before drafting those ideas. The drafting of ideas is the third part of the strategy. So, each time the sequence will be:

I read, you listen and sketch,
you talk with a partner,
you draft,
then we repeat the sequence.

Any questions? Remember that I am interested in seeing which aspects of this strategy most help you reconstruct and/or personalize the story.

She began reading the story—the students settled in. Some began sketching quite quickly. Others waited until she had read several paragraphs. A few started only after she had finished reading. As she read, the phrases from the introduction to the story were very noticeable. The students often murmured, nodded to one another, or paused in their sketching and looked up, trying to fit in another piece of the puzzle.

By the time she stopped reading, the setting of Antiques Alley ("several hundred stands and shops" with most wares "out on the ground", the exception being those "displayed in the glass cabinet") had been established and the proprietor with the bamboo ear spoon had been introduced. The class was working silently when she stopped reading. She wandered among them, giving more time for the sketch, before she interrupted.

TEACHER: Please turn and talk with your partner about what you were doing and what you were thinking about.

Acknowledge the affect as well as the cognitive.

Outlining the strategy allows learners to anticipate their more developed ways of thinking.

Moving among the students provides the teacher with divergent examples to connect across the class.

80

The room was instantly alive with refocused energy. She encouraged students who were reticent to share their actual sketch to talk about 'what was on their minds' and whether or not they were making mental pictures as she read. She also commented on the need to edit or re-sketch as new information was added.

TANYA: That really happened to me. I had all my antiques on tables like in Granville Island Market, then I had to arrow them down to the ground, then put in that glass cabinet. My picture kept changing.

Students practise visible, ongoing, reconstruction of knowledge.

TEACHER: It is interesting to note how movies we make in our minds are also made from our prior experience. When I say "stands and shops," you may quickly think "like a market", then the different information needed to make an Antiques Alley picture must deconstruct your earlier picture to allow for different information. Sometimes we notice that we don't do this. It feels safer or takes less energy to hang on to what we *want* to hear.

Share information on brain's processing.

This seemed to make sense to the students. They nodded to her and to one another.

TEACHER: Take another moment to talk, then shift your conversation to key concepts or what struck you about that part of the story that you would want to record in Box 2 on your paper.

They talked again, and I noticed many were now talking about her reference to the editing of the pictures.

Students use information presented by the teacher when it is relevant.

TEACHER: Before we continue, what suprised you about yourself, your partner, or the story?

STUDENTS: My partner drew little icons not a whole picture like me.

Prize diversity.

Your reading was so fast I could hardly keep up.

That guy with the bamboo ear spoon surprised me!

I thought I heard all the story, but Wade heard different stuff from me.

TEACHER: Well, let's continue. I shall keep on reading, and this time as you listen and sketch, notice if you follow your earlier patterns or if you change your way of thinking. Feel free to borrow any ideas you have heard or seen.

She continued reading, stopping when the purchaser had to finally decide whether or not to part with his money—whether or not the antique was fake. The students seemed more at ease this time and actively engaged with the story and with the strategy.

TEACHER: Before you talk with your partner, any comments?

STUDENTS: You read a great deal more that time.

Now that we've moved past the setting, it was easier to just sketch pieces.

I'm still not sure this helps me.

TEACHER: OK. Same sequence. Talk about what you were doing and what you were noticing. Then shift to key ideas to remember and draft those in Box 4.

Students talked again, pointing at their sketches, challenging one another, lending support to their attempts at representing their thinking in pictures. They were intrigued with the story. Many were predicting whether or not the incense burner was fake and if the expert dealer would buy it.

TEACHER: I'd like a show of hands before we continue. Who would take a risk and buy it? Who wouldn't? Defend your position to a nearby partner with whom you have not worked.

Everyone had an opinion.

Students move toward more independent choice.

TEACHER: I am going to finish reading. If you would like to sketch as I read, please do so. If you prefer to just listen, that's fine, too.

She read to the end. Several students sketched, but most 'just' listened.

TEACHER: A reflection before the bell goes. Please comment on your paper about your reactions to this strategy. What helped you make connections? Did you surprise yourself?

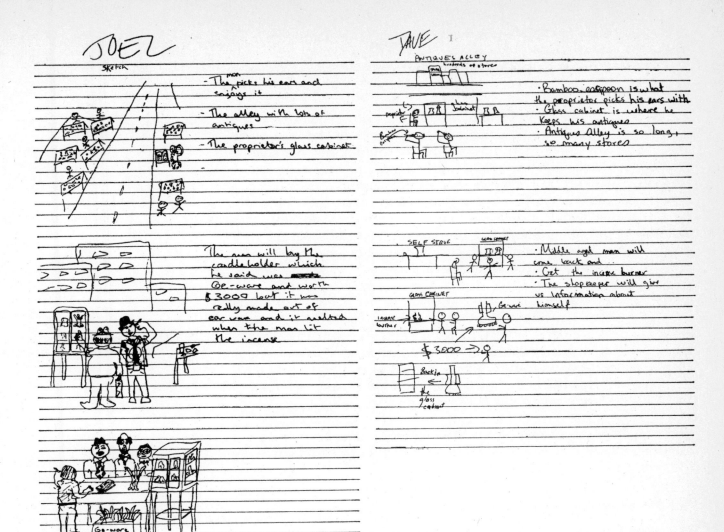

There was a real diversity in the responses of the students to this stategy. Their honesty reflected personal growth in their ability to look closely at themselves as learners and at what they needed next in learning. This growth toward independence is always encouraged.

WADE: The drawings and sketches helped me make connections.

SABRINA: I've tried a lot of different strategies to learn new ideas but personally, I am not very fond of the *Listen-Sketch-Draft* strategy at all. My thinking was awful. My ideas were unclear and I couldn't explain the picture I had drawn to myself. I don't mind brainstorming or the two column notes. Words are involved in that. I'm better with words than with drawings. I'd rather take notes any time over drawing my 'notes'. Next time, if possible can we stay with regular writing notes! I really tried my best to make the best of this strategy. But unfortunately it really didn't work for me. Next time, I think you should let each student do whatever strategy she or he feels most comfortable with.

BRENT: I noticed that I could get my ideas down quickly on the paper. I would usually listen for a while and pick out a few details and draw them. If I could remember small details about the major facts I could just fill them in wherever. The notes that I would write after drawing came easily because of the sketch. Doing this helps me with my concentration because I can draw and listen at the same time. I like the speed involved because I can't draw that well so my stick men will be enough to understand the whole picture.

TAMI: I think the *Listen-Sketch-Draft* was an OK idea but if you start drawing at the beginning, you don't hear the rest of the paragraph. But at the same time when we discuss it at the end everyone brings up different points so you get to hear about the rest of the story. I think this is better than just listening to you read the whole story but I would not like to do it every day.

This is definitely a reminder to us to extend the invitation to reflect, to be informed by what we are told, and to honor the diversity of the learners.

Practice is informed by student reactions and reflections.

The Next Class

The teacher began by discussing with the students what she had learned from their reflections on the strategy. They then worked in triads to determine the impact of the setting on the story. The students were asked to consider how much of this story was transferable to a different time and place, and how much was context specific. After the small group discussions, they wrote individually in response to the story.

Cross-Curricular Applications

1. *Social Studies*

   This strategy is useful in helping students make connections and identify with people and historical events. In response to an excerpt about William Lyon Mackenzie, who attempted to force representative government through armed rebellion, Tanis sketched and wrote the material that appears on the next page.

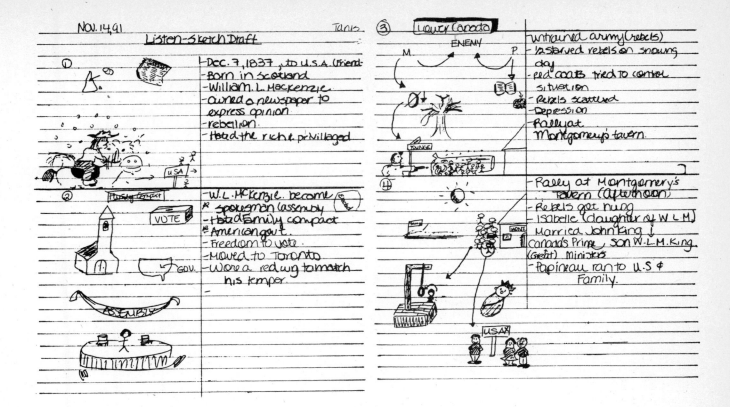

2. *Science*

   When studying magnets and electricity, the teacher read
   excerpts from the text and used *Listen-Sketch-Draft* to build key
   concepts with the students. Following this, the students
   conducted experiments.

3. *Physical Education*

   Using an adaptation of *Listen-Sketch-Draft*, students were asked
   to summarize, using minimum line drawings, key elements of
   soccer.

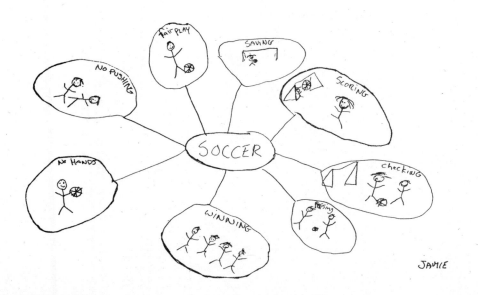

LISTEN-SKETCH-DRAFT

1. Divide response sheets into four or six boxes.

2. Read a section of text aloud while students sketch in Box 1 what comes to their minds as you are reading.

3. Students talk to one another about what they sketched and what they were thinking about.

4. Students talk to one another about what is important to remember from that part of the text.

5. Students write/draft what is important to them in Box 2.

6. Repeat the sequence.

7. Invite students to finish reading on their own.

8. Students reflect on what aspects of the strategy most supported meaning making.

9

ReQuest

The understandings of the disciplines represent the most important cognitive achievements of human beings. It is necessary to come to know these understandings, if we are to be fully human, to live in our time, to be able to understand it to the best of our abilities, and to build upon it.

— H. Gardner, *The Unschooled Mind*

Debriefing skills . . . are learned from the teacher's ability to perceive the differences in the interactive dialogue between questions and responses that call for examination of meaning and those that call for answers, and from the teacher's valuing of the examination of meaning as more important than answers.

— Centennial Case Study Project, *Cases for Teaching in the Secondary School*

I expect good reading and writing in which one process enriches the other, in which students' ideas and wonderings and questions invite risks, taking them to the outer edges of what they know and what they can do. I expect good reading and writing, in which process and product are woven tightly into literate tapestries of wonder and awe.

— L. Rief, *Creating Diversity*

As new information becomes apparent and as new knowledge comes into being, human understanding is expanded and deepened, and it becomes possible to further construct knowledge.

— Ministry of Education and Ministry Responsible for Multiculturalism and Human Rights, *The Intermediate Program: Foundations, Draft*

The grade ten social studies class had been studying the beginning of responsible government. As the class begins, they are being introduced to a new strategy, chosen to help them become more active, thoughtful readers.

TEACHER: Hello and welcome. Your starter for today is to think of three words that strike you as significant when you think of responsible government. Quickly jot these down. Then turn to your partner and negotiate your six words into three. Make these agreed-upon words into a *Concept Map*. Remember, this is a quick focus. Notice how effective you are at getting "tuned in".

Begin with an activity that helps the students bridge the last class and its content to the learning events of the present class.

The students shuffled about, finding papers, pens, friends, chatting quietly to one another, searching through past events to re-collect information relevant to this class. In five minutes, they had completed their Concept Maps, shared a couple with the entire class, and were beginning to work as a class unit rather than as individuals collected from a variety of other spaces.
   I noticed how easily the teacher did her 'house-keeping' tasks at this time, then circulated among the students, pulling in the recalcitrant learners, helping the wanderers collect and focus, valuing the effort required in such a quick task.

Management is fluid and respectful of the individual learner.

TEACHER: Today we are continuing our study of responsible government. I think the issues covered in our text are quite complex—maybe because our background knowledge is not as developed as it might be. I think this may be because we don't spend a great deal of time playing with this information, tossing it around in casual conversation to make it our own. I could be mistaken. Have you been talking about Lord Durham when you've been away from me?

Establish a purpose for using this strategy.

They smiled and rolled their eyes. Clearly, there was a climate of mutual respect and honesty. This teacher worked hard to bridge the curriculum content to the lives of the students, but accepted the responsibility for often making the first step in this bridge.

TEACHER: The strategy we are going to explore today is called *ReQuest* or *Reciprocal Questioning*. It is a strategy that is designed to help you process information in a text; it helps you work with the information and make it your own so that it is readily accessible when you want to draw on it in another context. It is based on the theory that efficient readers question themselves and the text as they read, and that they tend to ask themselves three general types of questions:

- on the lines—those answers that can be found by simply looking back at the text;
- between the lines—those answers that can be found by problem solving, inferring, or using the clues to build connections;
- beyond the lines or in your head—those answers that can be found by thinking of what you know already and putting this information to work.

Present an overview of the lesson.

We will read a portion of the text together, using the overhead, and ask these three types of questions to ourselves and to one another. We will do this in teams. I need a volunteer team of three or four members who think they could be the first group to question the rest of us.

Volunteers were numerous. She chose a representative sample: a student who was considered to be very thoughtful, a student who rarely handed in assignments, a quiet student, and a non-stop talker, quick retort student.

Heterogeneity is prized.

TEACHER: Since you four are going to take over my role as conductor at this time, you may want to begin by checking for clarification on the process and on the types of questions you will be asking and the types of responses you will be expecting.

Teacher moves quickly aside to encourage more dialogue.

The four students reviewed with the others the kinds of questions they would be asking. They laughed as they pushed their classmates to recall exactly the expectations of the questions and the type of thinking that would be required.

TEACHER: Let me remind you of the steps of the process. We will read the first section together from the overhead. Then we will cover the text for those of you who are responding—the group of four will ask you questions of this text section. If you need to look back, ask that the text be uncovered. Think of what you know each time and how you can use this to assist you in responding. Once it is evident that this section of text is clear, we will read on and change the role of questioner. You people will question these four and press their thinking.

DAVID: I want to start with an 'in the head' question. How would the majority of Canadians feel if the minority British form of commerce was imposed?

STUDENT: Mad.

DAVID: Tell me more.

STUDENT: Mad because they don't want to change to that system because they thought they wouldn't be treated fairly if they were all treated equally.

DAVID: OK. Anyone else?

STUDENT: It wouldn't happen because they wouldn't elect it and they are the majority.

Knowledge evolves through interaction with text, self, and others.

DAVID: But he's the governor and he can do what he wants.

STUDENT: That's not responsible.

The students were murmuring to one another. This first question had caused some new connections. It had also created more questions in the listeners and in the questioners. David was relentless in searching for support and evidence for theories proposed by his classmates.

MARK: This is 'on the lines'. What are the main points or arguments about the causes of conflict?

A number of students raised their hands. This seemed to be much easier.

STUDENTS: It was a struggle between the people.

He was splitting up the English and the French.

He was British and thought that even though there were less of them, they had superior commerce and industry so everyone should have to do it their way.

CARLY: This is 'in the head'. Why did Durham feel that the British commercial way of life was superior to the French agricultural way of life?

TEACHER: Interesting question. It seems to flow right out of Mark's 'on the lines' question.

Make connections explicit.

STUDENTS: Agriculture was by hand and it takes too long.

When it's commerce there's more people working and more systems—like big business.

DAVID: I've a sort of 'between the lines' question. You have to be able to figure this out. What is the difference between a commercial way of life and an agricultural way of life?

STUDENTS: Agriculture is digging in the dirt, commerce is selling stuff.

One is slow-moving country life, the other is the bustle of cities and big time.

GINA: This is 'on the lines'. What is Radical Jack's prediction of what would happen between the government and the people?

STUDENT: Easy. Conflict.

TEACHER: Interesting question. Notice how you assume that prediction is going to be 'beyond the text', but it isn't always. Sometimes the writer tells you what she or he assumes will happen. When you know the type of question being asked, you can more easily match an appropriate response. Gina was checking

The teacher's role is to clarify and extend reasoning.

to see what you *remembered*, not what you *thought*. And she didn't trick you! OK. We are shifting roles. We'll read on, then you can ask the questions and we will try and respond. I am going to join this team, in case they need some expertise!

The class groaned, then quickly and silently began to read. I noticed that in several cases, a reader naturally began reading aloud to a partner. This support allowed those ESL students and students who found the text particularly challenging to be a part of the thinking and the conversation, without being isolated. Other students turned to one another and asked for clarification on certain terms.

Question 1: OK you guys, 'on the lines'. What did Durham think had to be the way?

STUDENTS: They had to speak English.

Question 2: How would you feel if you were a Lower Canadien and someone gave you a national character?

What kind of question is it? . . . 'beyond the text' or 'in the head'.

STUDENTS: Mad because of the language.

Offended.

It assumes we have no national character.

Question 3: I think this is the second kind, 'between the lines'. Why does he want the French to be like the English?

TEACHER: It is often difficult to distinguish 'between the lines' and 'beyond the lines' questions. I tend to think of the 'between' being the kind of clue-type questions that detectives solve—the kind where you get several pieces of information and you try and weave them together to make something that makes sense. Then I think of 'beyond' questions as being predictions or new theories or opinions. Does that make sense? . . . Any responses?

STUDENTS: He thought it was a better way of life.

That's where he came from so its a natural thing to do.

Less work for him.

Question 4: I don't know what kind this is, but isn't there more than one country in Britain?

STUDENTS: No. They all speak English.

Yes. England, Scotland, and Wales.

Communities of learners look after one another.

Students quickly assume responsibility for extending the thinking.

91

TEACHER: Good. A *real* question. It will be your focus for next class. I'll want to know *how* you found out, too. Think of primary and secondary sources when you are searching.

The students jotted down the question in their notebooks. This pattern, linking one class to another, was well established. Many made eye contact with another and murmured, ''I know how I'll find out.''

TEACHER: Let's change the role of questioners one more time before we close. This is the last section we will read and talk about together, then you can finish it independently.

DAVID: This is a memory or 'on the lines' question. What are the three major religions that would be opposed to the Church of England? We'll pick them off one at a time, so be alert!

STUDENTS: Methodist
Catholic
Presbyterian

CARLY: This is probably 'beyond the text'. What are some of the reasons that the Church had control of the land?

STUDENTS: The settlers were mostly British and the English thought they were the best so Durham brought 'Church' people from England.

Because all the *rich* English people belonged to the Anglican Church and they were all members of the Family Compact.

MARK: Who are the Tories and who's their leader?

STUDENT: Mulroney.

A lot of laughter.

MARK: No, I meant at this time we are reading about.

STUDENT: Oh, you meant, 'between the lines'. Guess you should have told us or we would have been right!''

TEACHER: Good point, Brian. You have given us a natural break. You did well for a first time at *ReQuest*. Please finish the text on your own, then reflect for a few moments in writing on the impact of this strategy on your thinking and learning.

They quickly settled into reading, then reflecting. I was impressed with the on-task engagement of the students and with their ease at taking ownership of the lesson and personalizing the content.

Burning questions or purposeful inquiry links the content from class to class.

Knowing how to search is often as important as having the question.

Individual response after group work encourages development of personal understanding.

92

The Next Class

The stage was set with the focus question, "Is Britain more than one country?" The initial five minutes centered on a lively discussion of the students' responses and more importantly, how they found out. They moved from this focusing activity to a class discussion of the new strategy and what they could now remember as a result of the strategy. The teacher probed their thinking by continually searching for ways to make explicit the connections they had retained from the class. Was it asking the questions which helped you? Hearing someone's response that surprised you? Linking your ideas to those of someone else? Pushing a responder for extension or clarification? Reading the text?

The students completed more reading on their own, then worked with partners, in the role of John "Radical Jack" Lambton, the Earl of Durham, to prepare a written report for the British Government proposing solutions to the problems in Upper and Lower Canada in 1838.

Cross-Curriculum Applications

This strategy works easily with any curriculum area when the text is challenging and requires active reading for personal meaning-making (and understanding is crucial).

1. *English*
   Students worked with *ReQuest* to gain a personal understanding of Hamlet's "To be or not to be" soliloquy. This was followed by personal writing, "Chose an appropriate genre for your expression and show me that you understand Hamlet's soliloquy."

2. *Math*
   To promote understanding in problem solving, students used *ReQuest* to read the problem. Then, individually, they followed the write-up process as described in *The Interactive Mathematics Project*.

   Ms X, Ms Y, and Ms Z — an American, an English person, and a French person, not necessarily in that order, were seated around a circular table, playing a game of "Hearts". Each passed three cards to the person on her right. Ms Y passed three hearts to the American. Ms X passed the queen of spades and two diamonds to the person who passed her cards to the French person.

   Who was the American? the English person? the French person?

Problem Statement: restated in your own words.

Ms X, Ms Y, and Ms Z—an American, an English person, and a French person, but not in that order, were seated around a circular table playing ''Hearts.'' Each passed three cards to the person on the right. Ms X passed the queen of spades and two diamonds to the person who passed her cards to the French person. Ms Y passed three hearts to the American.

(Susan says the exact same problem but changes the order of the sentences.)

Process: How did you solve this?

Solution: Convince someone else that your solution works.

Ms X is American and passed to Ms Z who is English who passed to Ms Y who is French. Each person can only pass once. Since Ms Y passed to the American, she has to be French. Ms X has to be American because the American didn't receive the two diamonds and queen.

Evaluation: This was pretty easy, but keeps you thinking. I'm not sure if I'm right but it does work.

3. *Science*

Students in the lab were in groups of three and four. They were going to conduct an experiment with four unknown solutions to infer whether each is a chemical or a physical change. Prior to beginning the experiment, in their lab groups, they used *ReQuest* to read the text overview on characteristics of chemical and physical change.

REQUEST

1. Set the purpose for using the strategy.

2. Identify three kinds of questions: on the lines, between the lines, and beyond the lines.

3. Choose an initial team of four students to act as 'teachers' and question the other students.

4. Read a piece of the text on an overhead, then proceed with the questions.

5. Explain the type of question asked and encourage clarification and supportive evidence.

6. Read on in the text and change the role of the questioner.

7. Continue reading in this manner.

8. Individually, students reflect on the impact of this strategy on their meaning making.

9. After several sessions modeling in this way, students can work in teams of four, generating and responding to one another's questions.

10. Questions or key understandings can be written down to be used later as a study guide.

10

Responding With Key Ideas & Questions

The skill of asking divergent, or open-ended, questions is fundamental to the development of creativity. Divergent questioning . . . encourages several answers or possibilities . . . stimulates exploration of concepts . . . facilitates creative and critical thinking processes . . . promotes open-mindedness . . . consciously values individual differences . . . [and] provides challenge for all children.

— J. Dalton, *Adventures in Thinking*

. . . one of the most useful forms of qualitative inquiry, for my purposes, is found in literature . . . the writer starts with qualities and ends with words. The reader starts with words and ends with qualities.

— E. Eisner, *The Enlightened Eye*

People in dialogue also begin to observe the collective nature of thought . . . a 'kind of sensitivity' develops that goes beyond what we normally recognize as thinking. This sensitivity is a 'fine net' capable of gathering in the subtle meanings in the flow of thinking . . . collective learning is . . . vital to realize the potentials of human intelligence . . .

— P.M. Senge, *The Fifth Discipline*

Language and the world are understood through prediction — and prediction is the imagination at work. . . . Remembering, understanding, and learning are just different ways of looking at the imagination, or of talking about it.

— F. Smith, *to think*

The grade eight English students are grouped in pairs. A response sheet has been distributed to each student. In the two previous classes, the students had used seven excerpts from the text and the Building From Clues strategy to build an anticipation for the text.

TEACHER: You will recall these seven clues that you worked to prepare and how carefully you presented and supported your predictions using these clues.

The teacher revealed the clues on the overhead.

Frantically he thrashed around, seeking for an escape hatch.

The suffocating, fetid gases rushed out and in poured life-giving fresh, clean air.

He gazed dispassionately on their efforts to escape and made no attempt to help any of them.

. . . seeking an easier way past this heartbreaking setback.

His dulled mind could hold but one thought. Go on, go on.

Then the sky suddenly filled with screaming monsters, wheeling and diving over the staggering remnants of the band of travellers.

. . . he was content to rest, to enjoy the satisfaction of mission completed.

Repatterning as new information is added using prior knowledge and text information.

TEACHER: You will also recall generating vocabulary that you thought would be found in a story with those clues and the title ''Operation Survival''. The lists you created showed such diverse connections. Today, we are going to use a new strategy, *Responding with Key Ideas and Questions*, to interact with the text. How many of you think this is fiction? Nonfiction?

Reading/writing connections.

As the students justified their positions, I noticed how easily this group of students had come together as a class and how little time was lost on management. They knew their partners, had signed and dated their response sheets without direction, and had obviously expected to build on events from the last class. These established classroom routines gave more time for learning.

Quick review and extension prepares students to be on-task and ready to participate.

TEACHER: We're going to read like experts today. How would experts read a passage? What would go on inside their thinking? Jot your ideas in the first box on your response sheet, then share your ideas with your partner.

Talking through understandings builds both social competence and intellectual development.

Response Sheet

Strategy: Responding with Big Ideas

Name(s) *Mike*

Date(s) _____

What I Know		What do they make or do next?	What are you doing next?
Big Ideas			**Self-assessment about my big ideas**
-survival -Speed -keep moving -Escape -deserted spot - Freedom endangered -tiredness -close to -Teague mutant turtles -need water Death -Needs a -The attackers left Drink - Be careful -Close to end of Journey		*[sketch of capsule, sun, turtle — "capsule", "hurry"]*	Satisfied - descriptive - made sense
Questions			**advice for next time**
-What'll happen to him? -What happened to the other people? -If he'll make it.. -Where are the survivors? -Does he get water? -What do the missile look like -where is there? -Why is he a turtle? -Why is the story about a turtle?	It would be freaky and very hot especially for a turtle. It would be hard to climb with turtle feet. It would be refreshing though because he finnaly found water.	Have to push hard when you're weak Hot sand Screaming Monsters might have been vultures	Gather more ideas Ask more questions talk more **about my learning** - tough for me to get Big Ideas - A story can lead you on and then at the ends you get lost. - A story can sound like it's about one thing but then it turns out to be about another thing.

After a few minutes of talk, a collective list was generated on the chalkboard.

What Expert Readers Do . . .

- hook to what they know
- wonder, ask questions
- predict
- picture things they are reading
- paraphrase as they go
- talk to themselves
- read on to find out more
- react to the material
- do something with the information

TEACHER: As we read the text today, I'm going to ask you to stop and reflect a different way.

Complex engagement sets the stage for new discoveries.

The challenge excited the learners. They postured ready to work.

TEACHER: I need a volunteer to read the first third of ''Operation Survival'' while the rest of the class jots down important ideas. You may use words, sketches, webs . . . anything to hold on to what's important.

The open-ended response offers learners choices in both how and what they represent.

98

As the student read, some students began representing their ideas. Others listened or followed in the text first before responding.

TEACHER: Turn to your partner and talk about what was important to you. Also consider how you showed your ideas on paper.

Personal meaning deepens through the sharing of understandings.

The students talked through their connections. The teacher invited individuals to share key ideas, pressing for why the idea was important. She also asked the students to share how they decided what was important and what they noticed about how they represented their ideas.

Content, process, and product knowledge is constantly being developed.

TEACHER: We have used the *ReQuest* strategy a lot. Right under your Key Ideas box, jot down what you are wondering about. Notice what kind of questions you ask.
    What are you wondering? As we play with a few questions, be ready to offer your personal theory. Jason, let's hear one of yours.

Using familiar processes in new ways leads to flexible and independent use.

JASON: What happened to the other people?

Jason then fielded several responses because it was his question. New questions were posed. Each time the students responded directly to the questioner without involving the teacher. Meanwhile, the teacher looked for natural opportunities to press for elaboration and to model ways for extending and connecting varied responses.

The teacher steps aside and the student assumes control.

TEACHER: Turn your papers over. Put the word *Thinking* in the middle of your page. We're going to build a cluster showing the flow of thinking. Jot down, in circles, what you are noticing about your thinking. Share your ideas with your partner when you finish.

The students developed and quietly compared their responses.

TEACHER: We'll move a little more quickly now that you know the process. We need a new reader. . . . Thank you. . . . This time watch for innovations in how you show your key ideas. Notice how you approach the task.

The teacher encourages students to move beyond their safest response forms.

The students listened intently, capturing critical elements. At the end of the reading, they continued their personal response in silence for two or three minutes.

TEACHER: When you talk with your partner this time, notice key ideas and changes in your way of representing. Be alert for surprises.

STUDENT: Are those teacher minutes or real minutes?

They laughed. I recognized her dilemma in deciding to interrupt on-task conversation about the content of the curriculum.

TEACHER: Real minutes . . . What were the key ideas?

On the overhead projector, the teacher collected their key ideas. She accepted them all and then pushed for refinement.

TEACHER: What is a key idea?

STUDENTS: One that seems to hold onto something important.

One that gives me a real picture of what's going on.

When I can feel like I'm right there.

One that captures feelings.

An idea that makes me think of the conversation going on.

TEACHER: Look back at the selection we just read and generate questions. What are you wondering about before we read the final episode?

The students again generated and responded to one another's questions. You could feel them digging into the text for subtle details, reading and re-reading the passage for evidence. The teacher asked them to turn their papers over and document their thinking, this time using boxes or rectangles.

TEACHER: When we finish this last episode, your task will be to assess the way that you held on to or showed key ideas. Categorize your performances today. Did you feel you captured key ideas powerfully, competently, or are you still developing? Think about that as you show the key ideas in the last episode.

The students eagerly listened and composed their ideas. They were shocked when the teacher read the last paragraph. The author had caught them by surprise.

TEACHER: What are the key ideas?

She elicited responses from the quieter students. Subtle ways of expressing important ideas revealed how unique and diverse representation can be.

Honoring diversity shows the learners that there is no one right way to express thought.

TEACHER: In the self-assessment box, jot down what you noticed about your key ideas, then offer yourself some advice for the next time we use this strategy.

The students reflected with ease.

Self Assessment About My Key Ideas	Advice for Next Time
• I got suspense and excitement I'm satisfied • I feel mine was powerful because I can tell people about the story from my notes • I used both words and pictures I think mine was powerful because I remember the whole story • I used four quadrants to think it through	• learn big words so I know what things mean • go back to the clues • gather more ideas • ask more questions • look at drawing more like Jeff did • think more about the story when we are reading

TEACHER: What did you notice about your own learning?

These students were veterans of reflection.

STUDENTS: I had to really think, but I wanted to know how it would end.

I think this sheet was neat. I wouldn't have wanted to miss it. I can use it to study with.

I noticed I changed a lot. I think I did really well.

I was sure taken by surprise at the end.

I thought he was human. A story can sure lead you on.

TEACHER: Turn your papers over one last time. Using a shape of your own choice, illustrate how your thinking has developed. I noticed Jason has already started to show his thinking in clouds.

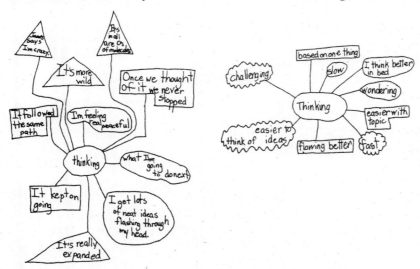

101

The Next Class

The students continued with the same partners. They chose the six most important ideas from the previously read story, "Operation Survival". Using these ideas, they created a *Concept Map*.

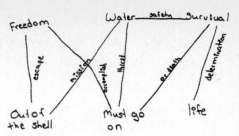

Cross-Curricular Applications

1. *Physics*

   The teacher put a word problem on the chalkboard and invited students to write down and share key ideas in solving the problem. Triads generated questions. Some groups focused on questions to clarify their thinking and others posed questions to challenge everyone's thinking. Students solved a similar problem independently, explaining and assessing their understandings.

2. *Science*

   The teacher orchestrated a series of demonstrations related to the digestive system. After each demonstration the students, in teams of five, positioned themselves at the chalkboard and identified key ideas and posed questions for other groups. The teacher modeled how to turn their developed understandings into a *Concept Map*.

3. *Mathematics*

   Students solved equations using the key ideas and questions to talk through their understandings.

4. *Social Studies*

   In a unit on changes in the Japanese culture, students clustered key ideas from a *National Geographic* article and a set of slides. After each portion, students collaboratively generated questions. They developed a group *Concept Map* to show understandings.

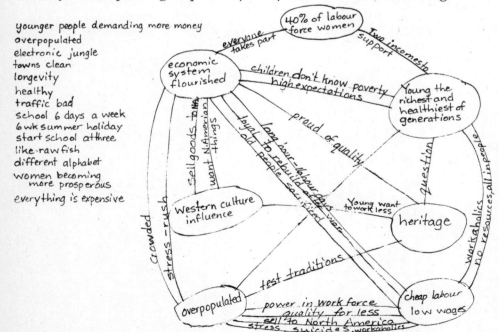

RESPONDING WITH KEY IDEAS

1. Students are in pairs.

2. Students reflect on how experts think as they read.

3. As the teacher reads a passage, students listen and collect key ideas.

4. With partners, students compare their key ideas and their representation of these ideas. Responses are networked beyond the pairs.

5. Students collaboratively generate questions they have about the next passage.

6. Students use modified *ReQuest* to answer some of their questions.

7. Students process several additional passages developing criteria for effective *key ideas* and *questions.*

8. Students assess, based on developing criteria and reflect on themselves as learners.

11

From Thinking Bubbles to Concept Maps

Measuring for each individual is being accumulated and modified operationally in the course of the discussion . . . each individual makes what he can of the discussion in light of his own individual experience, which, although having common touchstones with others is, nevertheless, unique.

— A. Wilkinson & L. Stratta, *Listening and the Teaching of English*

Humans have the capacity to experience the world in a multitude of ways and the inventiveness to represent their experience in forms that do them justice. To take this idea seriously . . . is to recognize that cognition is wider than language.

— E.W. Eisner, *Taking a Second Look: Educational Connoisseurship Revisited*

Debriefing . . . means helping each student discover what he or she has felt, thought and experienced during the instructional activity . . . experiences can have a powerful impact on individual goal-setting and conceptualization. Debriefed experiences increase this impact . . .

— D.A. Sanders & A. Sanders, *Teaching Creativity Through Metaphor*

Interpersonal intelligence involves awakening and utilizing capacities such as collaborating with other people, negotiating, compromising, building on another's ideas, willingly listening, and the 'give and take' of forming group consensus.

— D.G. Lazear, *Seven Ways of Knowing*

The bell rang to begin the class. With no 'call to order', the teacher picked up his copy of Singularity *by William Sleator and quietly began reading. I was surprised at how quickly the students settled into listening. After two or three paragraphs, he stopped.*

TEACHER: You already know a great deal about the two main characters, Harry and Barry. This morning, we'll work with that knowledge in three different ways. I'd like you to notice how much more you come to know about Harry and Barry as we do this. Then, because we know that you can do more than one thing with your brain at once, as we move from one process to the next, also notice your thinking. What is it that helps you make connections?

He divided the class into two groups and moved the students into partners within each group. The configuration surprised the class. They were very familiar with a range of interaction patterns. This one, however, was new to them.

TEACHER: Talk is such an important tool. Sometimes we underestimate its power. With each strategy we use today, we will use talk in a different way. Actually, we'll use words and our multiple intelligences to reveal our understandings.

The students were very familiar with the use of their intelligences. They had often reflected on how their capacities were developing using Gardner's Seven Intelligences as a framework.

TEACHER: Partners on this side of the class will focus on Harry during the first two strategies. Partners on the other side will focus on Barry. For the last strategy, we'll all focus on both characters. . . . Take three minutes and explore with your partner what you remember about your character. This conversation with a partner is your first strategy.

When the three minutes were up, he asked for volunteers to call out what they had uncovered about Harry or Barry.

TEACHER: Just as I thought. You have a lot of information about these two. Hang onto that information and consider a second strategy. This strategy is called *Thinking Bubbles* and it requires you to think like a cartoonist. Remember how to show thoughts in a cartoon as compared to speech.

On the overhead, he drew a circle to represent a character's head, then elicited from the students an example that illustrated the use of thought bubbles and of speech bubbles.

TEACHER: Review in your mind what your character has thought thus far in the novel and what he has said. Again, working with your partner, think like a cartoonist, draw his head, and show the

"Providing students with a repertoire of cognitive and meta-cognitive skills and strategies that will enable to them to use the knowledge efficiently in meaningful contexts." Marzano et al. (1988)

". . . intelligences work in combination. All of us possess these intelligences and all of us can use them productively." Gardner (1990)

Focus conversation to activate prior knowledge.

Sketching often helps students find the language they need to talk.

kinds of thoughts that reveal your character's personality and the talk that would reveal his particular qualities. Try to show your character as clearly and with as much evidence as possible.

For the next ten minutes the students collaborated, negotiating what would fully represent their character's thoughts and language.

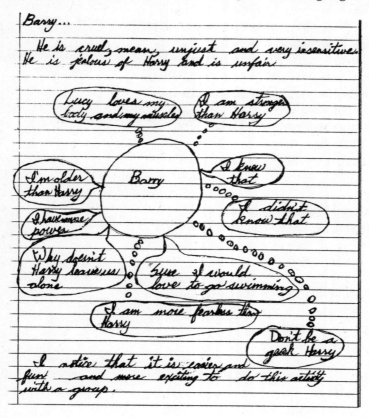

TEACHER: Before we hear about what you and your partner have accomplished, I'm interested in what you noticed about your thinking when you used this strategy. Reflect in your learning log.

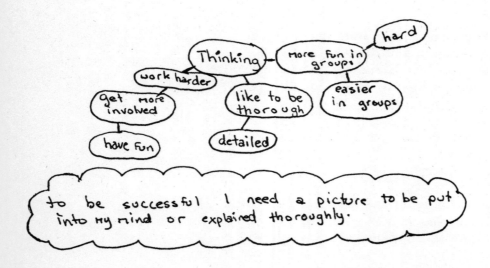

This again engaged the students. After a brief, individual response, the teacher heard from the students.

PATRICK: I liked this activity because when I drew the thinking I didn't have to remember all the words. I just drew it, and then we could go into more detail.

For most students, this does not feel like 'work'.

SAMARA: I noticed that I was able to come up with a lot more ideas with a partner than if I'd been on my own.

JODIE: My own personal thinking was a lot better flowing. When I worked with Samara on thinking bubbles her ideas triggered me into going deeper into words and phrases and finding meaning for the situation.

BROOKE: A partner and more than one way of learning made it easier to learn and reflect on the subject.

JON: It's better to do the bubbles with both thinking and talking because it reminds you of different things in the book and it shows more of his personality.

TEACHER: Did you notice a difference in your thinking when you worked with *Thinking Bubbles* compared to when you talked with your partner but didn't draw and write?

Again, he had pressed the students into considering the different ways they made meaning and which of these ways was most effective for each of them. He encouraged them to notice their diversity.

TEACHER: Partners who used *Thinking Bubbles* to show Harry will now have an opportunity to meet with a Barry partnership and compare your presentations. Feel free to add details to one another's cartoon and to ask for clarification or elaboration.

This talking has a real purpose and real audience.

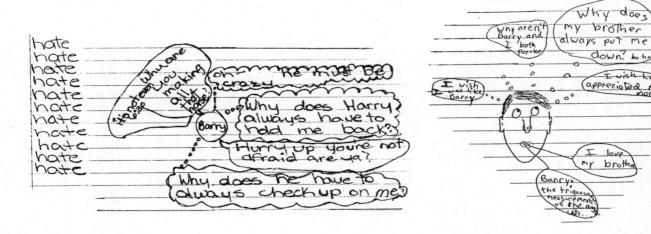

107

The students easily moved into sets of four. I noticed that they made frequent reference in their conversations to 'what worked' or was really effective. I gathered that this was a group that was comfortable with the ongoing development of criteria for success.

TEACHER: You have two Harry experts and two Barry experts in each group. You'll now regroup so you have one Harry and one Barry ready to work together. This will be the grouping for the third strategy, *Concept Mapping*.

He distributed another piece of paper to each new pair.

TEACHER: Your job is to brainstorm a list of the key ideas or important information about either of these two characters. This information does not have to be shared information. Write your list down the side of your page. From this list, you will build a *Concept Map* that represents how the relationship of Harry and Barry is the essence of the story.

The students had worked with Concept Mapping before. Once they had generated their lists, they moved quickly to drawing circles on the page, placing key ideas in the circles, and searching for evidence to link the key concepts. This evidence was drawn from the story and from their response to events, characters, and places in the story.

TEACHER: Let's hear some of your connections.

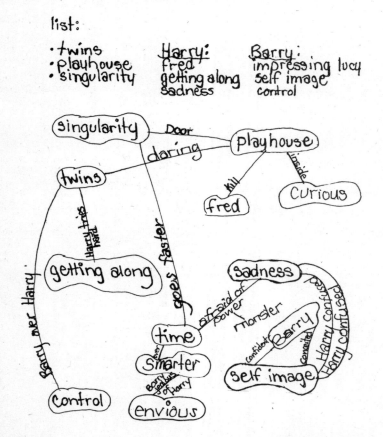

The students presented and substantiated their links. After each response, new connections were shared. The class ended with the students reflecting on the three different ways they had talked and represented their understandings. For homework, individuals were to finish reading the text.

The Next Class

The class began with a brief group reconstruction of the events of the final three chapters and personal responses to these events. As a group, they established criteria for powerful character representations. Criteria included:

- evidence from text;
- connection to experiences audience understands;
- character vignettes in a variety of contexts.

Individually, they chose their form to represent Harry or Barry. Forms included *Thinking Bubbles*, mime, soliloquy, or writing.

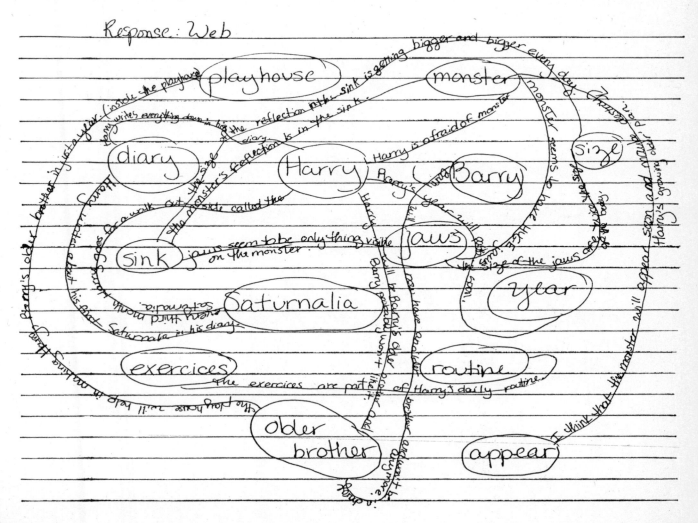

Response: Web

Cross-Curricular Applications

1. *Social Studies*
   Pictures of the Great Depression were studied in a *Gallery Walk*. Students created *Thinking Bubbles* to represent understandings of the time.

2. *Physical Education*
   Thinking Bubbles were used to represent student reactions in a variety of situations in which they were well-prepared or ill-prepared for self-defence.

3. *Art*
   At the end of a study, students created a set of Mona Lisa drawings in which her thinking reflected changes through the ages. Later, students chose an artist to investigate and used *Thinking Bubbles* to show elements of the artist's life and style.

4. *Mathematics*
   After a study of percentages, students first used imaging to picture themselves buying a used car, and then used *Thinking Bubbles* to demonstrate the car salesperson/buyer interaction. In order to demonstrate their ability to compute with percentages, at least three different offers had to be presented by the student and countered by the sales person.

5. *English/Poetry*

After a reading of ''The Love Song of J. Alfred Prufrock''
by T.S. Eliot, the students were asked to show that they
understood the tensions in the poem with a sketch. Josh's
picture clearly shows his understanding of the tensions of
Prufrock's thoughts.

6. *Science*

Prior to final exams, the students were asked to reflect with
Thinking Bubbles on a key event for them.

THINKING BUBBLES

1. Recall with students how a cartoon shows thought and speech.

2. After having experienced a character or group of characters, students demonstrate an understanding of the character by working like a cartoonist.

3. Encourage students to move beyond the text in their use of inner speech or thought.

4. Students work alone or in partners.

5. This strategy can be used while reading to monitor character change.

12
Editing Without Agony

One kind of writing that . . . promotes substantive engagement is the position paper . . . such writing tasks promote student "ownership" because they afford students considerable flexibility concerning the content they cover and the views they express.

— M. Nystrand & A. Gamoran, *Student Engagement: When Recitation Becomes Conversation*

Clustering taps the . . . curious, open-ended, flexible, pattern-seeking, design mind allowing us to play with language, ideas rhythms, images, sounds . . . creatively before committing ourselves to a fixed vision of a tentative whole, enabling us to begin writing easily and coherently.

— G.L. Rico, *Writing The Natural Way*

Whenever students write cooperatively, they seem to be able to unconsciously teach others a great deal about writing and how to make it better . . . the teacher's role is to make sure that the learners have the opportunity to clarify . . . to make observations . . . to form and test hypotheses and to reflect on the results.

— G. Boomer, *Fair Dinkum Teaching and Learning*

. . . students of all ages should evaluate and monitor their processing at every stage of solving a problem. The teacher's role would be . . . to help students establish criteria . . . and to make them aware of their own metacognitive processing . . . so they will eventually internalize the process.

— R.J. Marzano et al., *Dimensions of Thinking*

The grade nine students are nearing the end of a media investigation. In the last class, they analyzed functions and forms of radio stations. Today they will take on the role of volunteers at a public community radio station in dire need of funds. Their task will be to persuade a government agency to award their station a grant. The students are grouped in pairs.

TEACHER: Good morning. You have been chosen to represent your radio station. Your assignment is to persuade a government agency to fund your station. If you are successful, the station will continue. We'll work through a process called *Editing Without Agony* to help you. By the end of this class, your argument needs to be drafted.

The study is elevated to real-life applications.

A serious tone was set within the first few seconds.

TEACHER: What do you know about the economy in British Columbia today?

CHRIS: There's not much money.

SARAH: Cutbacks are affecting everything.

The teacher held up a recent issue of the local paper featuring the effects of a failing economy and read several of the headlines.

Set a larger context.

TEACHER: In this climate of recession, you need to determine the unique aspects of your station's service and to convince a panel holding on to public funds that your station warrants financial support.
   To warm up, I will image the information you investigated last class. As I read the selected words, use the *Four Quadrants of a Thought* to help you recall unique qualities of your station.

Working in role transfers the design responsibility to the students.

The teacher drew four quadrants on the overhead projector, had students help her label each part, then invited the sets of partners to use the organizer to talk for two minutes about their radio knowledge.

language	images
physical sensations	emotions

TEACHER: What did you notice about your thinking as you used the organizer to talk through your understandings?

STUDENTS: It really helped. I thought of way more than just the community stations.

   I had lots of strong feelings about my station.

Build ownership and commitment to learning.

I could hear us planning the drug campaign. We were worried.

TEACHER: As I read, notice the details . . .

- see yourself walking into your station . . . [2-3 second pause]
- hear the people talking about the station's audiences
- notice plans to appeal to those audiences
- feel the concern for reaching the community
- hear critical needs the station must address
- see yourself at a finance meeting
- hear the budget needs
- notice people voting you in charge of persuading the government to fund the station
- when I count to three, turn to the person beside you and tell them what's important about your station and why it should be funded
- 1 . . . 2 . . . 3

A two-or three-second wait allows the brain time to process.

The image supports personal connections.

Everyone talked as insiders in the experience. After several minutes, the teacher assumed the role of a talk-show host.

TEACHER: With us in the studio today are volunteers from a host of community radio stations. They have an incredible responsibility. Ladies and gentlemen, each of these young people has been elected to convince a government agency to award their station a grant. We've invited them here today to hear their station's offerings— what makes them unique and worthy of financial support.

Building belief through role play.

The teacher moves beside a student and begins interviewing.

TEACHER: Sir, what's unique about your situation?

JAMIE: We have an anti-drug program running within the community and we sponsor special events like the Handicapped Olympics. Without our support, these events might disappear.

Smiles and nods from the students showed recognition of persuasive ideas.

TEACHER: Thank you, Jamie. We certainly wouldn't want to see those supports lost in your community. Good luck with your appeal.

The teacher extended her hand to another student.

DAVID: We are struggling for money. We have counsellors at the station who host community phone-in shows and they have drop-in times at the station. People come in and discuss their problems with trained people. The community depends on us for jobs. We also host fundraising events where the money goes to the needy and the homeless within our community.

TEACHER: Thank you, David.

She continued to interview various station spokespeople, then invited the students to reflect on their thinking in role. She moved among the partners. The class talked reflectively. As she invited responses, she made no comment except for "thank you" to acknowledge the response.

JEANETTE: I was searching for really important things that the station does. It felt so real.

EVE: As people talked, I got new ideas that I hadn't even thought of before. Some of them didn't connect with what we were talking about.

HARJINDER: I've got ideas now.

SARAH: The multicultural idea is so real for our community now. We know it will work.

Energy and commitment for the task were high. The students were ready to express their ideas on paper.

TEACHER: In the *Editing Without Agony* strategy, we write individually, stop, listen to a few drafts to refine criteria that we developed for powerful writing, write collaboratively, stop and refine our criteria again, then write individually one last time. I know it sounds like a lot of steps. Once you've experienced it, you won't believe the power in the process.

Let's begin by revisiting the criteria we established during our last writing focus. These criteria were developed for informative writing.

"In dialogue, a group explores complex difficult issues from many points of view . . . The result is a free exploration that brings to the surface the full depth of people's experience and thought . . ." Bohm, in Caine & Caine (1991)

- organized and focused
- ideas flow, connect to each other
- points explained with details
- short and to the point
- believable

Your writing today will be to persuade. Will we need to change any of these criteria before we begin?

HARJINDER: Something about hooking to your audience if you want to convince them.

TEACHER: Let's add it. . . . Each write we do today will only be approximately five minutes. Next time we use the process, we might take two or three classes. That will depend very much on our purpose and audience. You are charged with the responsibility of convincing a committee to fund your station. Clustering might help you to generate ideas.

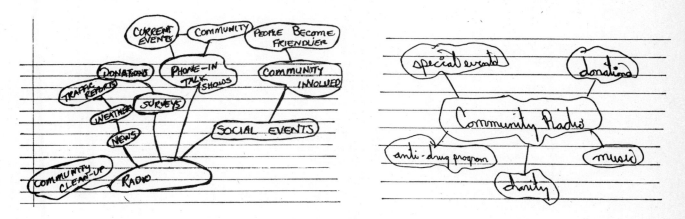

The students' familiarity with clustering and their flexible use of connecting processes make the transition into writing very smooth.

TEACHER: You have about eight minutes, three to play with ideas and five to write a beginning draft.

The teacher sat down to begin her draft. Sometimes she worked at the chalkboard or on the overhead and sometimes the students did. Everyone was engaged in the process. As the observer, I also wrote. My radio understandings were limited, but I certainly had knowledge of the impact of radio in my community.
  Silence enveloped the writers.

TEACHER: Five seconds . . . Read your draft out loud to yourselves. I know this feels funny but you need to stand back from your writing and hear what you have to say. Your whole brain will be engaged and you will know if it really says what you want it to say. Feel free to cross out things you don't want and add new ideas.

The students looked a little uncomfortable about reading out loud at the same time. The teacher began and everyone engaged. Deletions and additions followed.

TEACHER: Underline a part that you know works . . . a powerful part you wouldn't give up. Now, let's hear a few of these examples:

The students listened intently.

TEACHER: What did you notice about those passages?

SARAH: They were believable.

TEACHER: Now we are going to listen to a number of drafts to refine our criteria. Your job is to see yourself as a committee member deciding on the stations that will receive grants. As you listen, notice what touches you and what works.

The audience is established and the listening is structured.

The students assumed facial expressions and body positions of authority as they listened to a draft.

DRAFT #1

Dear Sirs,   May 28/92
I'm writing to you from M.R. a small town near Vancouver. Our community stations provides activities for the mentally handicapt and the mentally ill. We provide supervisors to take them through our station and show them how it works. We also provide jobs to do for them like making flyers promoting our station. The reasons for including the mentally handicapt and the mentally ill in our community is because there are many of them in our community with nothing to do all day they just sit around in homes or with caretakers and there bored. Also our program has a slow relaxing, enjoyable, beat to listen to all day long with no comercials.

TEACHER: Talk to your partner about what worked, what caught your attention, and what struck you. You are both on the committee.

The students discussed the draft, and the teacher pressed them for convincing details. They listened to four drafts; generally partner discussion was followed by collective sharing. The adapted set of criteria evolved from the study of the drafts.

- original ideas
- commitment from the people
- tightly written, not always short
- ideas flow and the order builds
- something that hooks you
- logical, believable

118

TEACHER: You and your partner have a new task. You both represent one station. In the room, we now have fourteen stations
appealing to the government for funding. Look at your drafts.
Think about what you've heard. Your job is to secure a grant for
your community radio station by writing a collaborative draft. You
have about five minutes.

*Some partnerships wrote immediately, while some talked for a length
of time before writing.*

TEACHER: Assume your role as a committee member responsible for
granting funding. We'll listen to a few collaborative drafts. Your job
is to notice what is powerful and what works in the application.

*The students listened intently. They raised their hands to offer
evidence of power.*

TEACHER: What worked?

GARY: Making the community a better place.

TEACHER: What could you call that in terms of criteria? What is the
author showing the committee?

*How criteria look and
sound must be explicit
to students.*

GARY: Information that shows the money is used for a good
          cause.

CHRIS: It shows evidence of understanding community needs.
          The author's voice convinced me. I felt like I was right
          there and responsible.

*The class discussed what that might be called. Understanding the
needs of others and author's voice were added to the list.*

TEACHER: What else worked?

DAVID: Reaching out to the community and making us feel the
          consequences.

*After a brief discussion, awareness of consequences and appeal to
audience were added to the list.*

TEACHER: Let's hear another draft.

*Two more drafts were read. Students articulated what was powerful
about each one. Criteria were refined.*

TEACHER: You've written individually. You worked collaboratively, testing out ideas. Now, a moment of truth. You, alone, are responsible for your station's funding. Of the eight criteria we have developed, choose four or five that you value in your persuasion. Use the unique qualities of your station to convince the committee to award a grant. You have five minutes.

Everyone began writing, reaching for words to convince. After five minutes, the teacher stopped the students briefly.

TEACHER: Great! In one hour, we have engaged in a very sophisticated editing process. The next time we use it, you will have much more extended time to play with and refine your ideas. I'm also interested in how this transfers into your author's circle in personal writing. Look at what you have in your draft. Do a quick assessment offering support for your decision and a reflection on your learning today.

The class read their drafts, referred to the criteria developed, and assessed the familiar categories: Powerful, Competent, Developing, and Undeveloped. The class ended with individuals sharing their assessments and reflections.

Continually build knowledge and application of process.

- My writing and thinking have changed through the whole activity. Mine is *powerful* because I use a lot of issues that are present in our community.
- My writing is believable and to the point, powerful, one main idea, supported.
- I noticed that my writing has changed dramatically. The more I thought, the more powerful issues came to mind.
- Powerful. I think my letter is powerful because I offer many programs and I talk about how the station is isolated. The more drafts I did, the better my writing got. I thought of more ideas.
- I noticed that my writing changed when we went through it about six times.
- I think my letter is powerful because I provide many supporting facts for my arguments, such as the fact we receive no other media. My thinking improved as I went along. My writing was refined.
- I noticed I was thinking about what's good for the station and the people. My second draft was better than my first.

The Next Class

The students reflected on the *Editing Without Agony* process and then prepared to create advertisements that would appeal to their particular radio audiences. They used the new editing process to revise their ads.

Cross-Curricular Applications

1. *English Literature 12*

   The students' task was to describe the structure of a Shakespearean five-act play, *MacBeth*, as it pertained to the tragic hero. They began and ended the study by identifying the elements of a tragedy. The pre- and post-samples provided rich data for performance assessment. The students individually wrote introductions. They developed criteria for an effective introduction using thesis statements based on their reading. Students then collaboratively wrote, listened to drafts, and defined and refined criteria. They wrote a final draft. One student reflected:

   > I used to be afraid of criticism. By learning to self-evaluate, I realize it's not criticism in a negative sense. It is simply a way to help me to do my best.

   The teacher noticed intensity in the students' desire to continue to write. They all showed self-confidence and worked together as a team. The writing improved dramatically.

2. *Law 12/English 8*

   In preparation for a mock trial, the students assumed the role of the accused in *The True Story of the Three Pigs by A. Wolf* as told by Jon Scleszka. They used the *Four Quadrants of a Thought* to gather data for use in idea sketches.

Students clustered and drafted an argument in role as the wolf facing the jury. They listened to the drafts in role as jury members. Criteria for persuasive argument were developed. Students reflected on their learning.

A grade eight English class followed the same sequence. They went on to write collaboratively, refine criteria, and write a final argument. The class ended with each student assessing their drafts and reflecting on their own learning.

DRAFT 1

I'm sorry... maybe what I did was less than heroic, but I was merely trying to make my Grandmother's birthday great. It may be her last you know. I was just trying to be neighbourly when that little porker insulted the person I hold dearest, my grammy. Now isn't that just more proof that I'm a caring and loving wolf.

Yours sincerely and sorrowfully
A. WOLF

made me think deeper.

Mike   DRAFT 2

I'm innocent I tell you, I've proven it twice, why are you putting me through this? I'm just a poor wolf trying to put my life together again. I'm on the edge. Yesterday sweet old Potsy Porker egged my house because of all this. And dear old Granny plunged off the Canadian National Tower headfirst onto a tack all because she was ashamed of me. I've been through enough punishment, just let me go.

Thanks,
A. Wolf

Collaborative

DRAFT 3

Mike

Dear Upstanding members of the Society, I am sorry, so sorry, very sorry, all this happened because I merely wanted to get a single measly cup of sugar. As for the pigs, I only ate them because they were dead, my dear sweet old granny always said that there are people dying from starvation in Ethiopia and other third world countries. I was simply defending their honour when I did it. No food shall ever go to waste in my presence. Now don't go thinking that I do this all the time because I don't, it has never happened before. Now to clear up a common misconception. Some of you think that I did it in cold blood just because I was drawn as a heinous psychotic murderer by the newspapers. Did you believe the national inquirer when they

said Elvis was reincarnated as a cabbage patch kid? NO! I think not. Is there any difference with me? I think you should reach down into your heart and I think you will find that you can't in any way find me guilty. I think you all know I'm innocent. Thank you.

Yours sincerely and sorrowfully
A. Wolf

Powerful: compared to facts made it seem like the right thing to do.

122

3. *English*

The students were writing in role based on their individual reading. Criteria for powerful responses were developed using a professional example of the form they were using. After developing criteria, students wrote. In groups of four, drafts were shared. Each student read his or her draft. After each reading, the group discussed the draft, then wrote notes to the author noting:

- three criteria the writing met;
- two questions they had as listeners of the writing or of the author;
- one thing the author might change.

The feedback was exchanged. In the next class, students drafted again, making changes only as they chose, based on peer responses.

4. *Physics: Problem Solving*

Students solved a problem individually. Several students volunteered to explain to the class their solution. The class listened, noticing what worked well. Partners worked collaboratively on a new problem. Pairs moved into squares to share their approach to solution finding. Teams presented powerful ways they used to solve the problems. Individuals again tried a problem on their own and reflected on their finding and approach to the solution.

5. *Math: Exponent Laws*

Once the students were familiar with explaining their understandings, the teacher created a "People Search" (Bellanca & Fogarty, 1990). With six problems to solve, the students moved around the room to find people who could solve the problem and explain their approach. The student listening had to demonstrate understanding before the person explaining could sign the box.

Jeanne

Find someone who can calculate one of the following, and then explain the law.

1. $\dfrac{a^5}{a^2} = a^3$

law 2 *Jennifer*

2. $x^7 + x^3$

x^{10} Law #1

Karen

3. $(2x^3y^2)^3$

$= 8x^9y^6$

Law #3

Dana

4. $\left(\dfrac{a^2}{a^2b^3}\right)^4$

$\dfrac{a^8}{a^8b^{12}} = \dfrac{1}{b^{12}}$ Law #4

MES

5. $\dfrac{(2a^2)^3}{8a^6}$

Stacie

Law #5

6. $(4a^2)(2a^3)^2$

$4a^2 \times 4a^6$ Law 3.

$16a^8$

DAlige

The students reflected on the following questions.

- What did you do well in the "People Search"?

  I did #6 and #2 well. I completed my sheet because I got up and moved around.

- How could you have been more successful at this task?

  I could have helped explain a certain question to someone.

- Did the exercise help you gain a better understanding of exponent laws? How did it help?

  Yes, although I wasn't here it helped me remember from last year. It helped me to remember when to multiply exponents, etc...

- Did you like this activity? Why? Why not?

  Yes... I do like these kinds of exercises because I feel it's easier to learn when you're having fun and getting not only the teacher to help you, but the other students in your class to help and share their ideas.

EDITING WITHOUT AGONY

1. Read an image to set the context for learning and to link the content.

2. As a talk-show host, interview students in role about the content.

3. Students reflect with a partner on what and how they remembered.

4. Review criteria for effective writing and revise to fit form.

5. Students write individually.

6. Students identify and share powerful parts of their writing.

7. Several drafts are read to the whole class and partners discuss 'what worked.'

8. Criteria are refined based on 'what worked', purpose, and form.

9. Partners write collaboratively.

10. Several drafts are read again, critiqued, and criteria refined.

11. Students individually choose four or five criteria that are most relevant to them and write.

12. Students self-assess, based on their criteria.

IMAGE–CLUSTER–DRAFT

1. The teacher reads an image to students to re-establish the context and establish personal meaning.

2. Each student listens and clusters the connections that comes to his or her mind.

3. Students can double-circle key ideas/concepts/words from their cluster.

4. Students talk to a partner about their cluster or their thinking.

5. Students may be interviewed in role to build belief and relevance with the content.

6. Students continue the cluster, then draft a written response.

13

Frames for Connecting

. . . independent learners are able to stand back and look at the task which is set, analyze it, and identify several possible strategies for completing it. Then, as they engage in the task and try out selected strategies, they reflect on how well a particular strategy is working . . .

— G. Bull & M. Anstey, *Achieving independent learning: Drawing genre and process together*

When we think we try to make connections and see patterns, which will lead us to interpret the significance of whatever it is that we are thinking about in ways that had not occurred to us before.

— P. D'Arcy, *Making Sense, Making Meaning*

Students are now charged not with acquiring and remembering knowledge, but with making it, with crafting it out of the raw material of their experience, the text's, and their discourse with other students, teachers, and writers.

— R.E. Probst, *Literature as Exploration and the Classroom*

In the classrooms I visit, teachers are trying to design assessment tasks that explicitly invite students to make connections; we also collaborate with the students to develop criteria that reflect this focus.

— S. Jeroski, *Learner-focused Assessment: Helping Students Grow*

TEACHER: My goal in this next hour is to introduce to you three different ways of thinking about or reacting to experiences. This is simply an introduction. As we continue to work with these 'frames', you will be asked to reflect on which frame seems most appropriate to you in a variety of contexts. You will also eventually choose one of these 'frames' to show me that you understand a new piece of text.

Set the larger context for learning for the students.

I believe that we are capable of thinking of several things at the same time, and are capable of dealing with both complexity and ambiguity as we learn. Do you agree?

The students responded with nods and/or puzzled looks.

TEACHER: Well, looks to me as if some of you are willing to trust me and run with it. Good. Since you are powerful thinkers, I hope that you will participate on several levels:

Move beyond an activity to encourage thinking and processing on several levels simultaneously.

- first, by doing the activities as I present them;
- second, by noting how you feel about each change, and how easily you connect with the different processes;
- third, by noticing if the patterns of your thinking and learning change as you progress.

It is like changing channels on a T.V. You recognize the 'clicker syndrome', I'm sure — I'm the one who has the clicker today.

Relate new experiences to known facts.

We are observing a grade twelve English class. The thirty students are watching with varying degrees of suspicion as the demonstration teacher works to establish a relaxed climate, while letting them know her long- and short-term plans for the processes she is about to introduce. We teachers know that she is planning to teach poetry. The students are not yet aware that this is to be a poetry lesson. I wonder when she'll tell them.

TEACHER: Something that really intrigues me is how the brain works. I am constantly searching to learn more about it. Many researchers are discovering good news—that there are things we can do in school to make learning easier for everyone. Is there anyone here that doesn't think this is truly good news? This is one of your channels, remember. Notice if this first strategy helps you learn.

Model yourself as a learner.

I am going to give you a word. I want you to do several things when you hear my word. First, I want you to notice what first pops into your mind. Then I want you to let your thinking flow, but still remember what came first. Try to resist the urge to share your thinking. You will have a chance to do so in a few minutes. You do not have to write anything down.

OK. My word is 'week-end.'

Silence reigned for about a minute, then she began prodding.

TEACHER: What did you first think of?

STUDENT: Work.

TEACHER: Tell me about 'work'.

STUDENT: I have to go to work this week-end.

TEACHER: Was it like a word association? I said 'week-end' and you immediately thought 'work'?

STUDENT: Yes.

She wrote 'work' on the board.

TEACHER: Someone else.

STUDENT: No school.

TEACHER: Yes, and I saw you. You smiled as soon as I said the word 'week-end'.

'No school' went on another part of the board.

TEACHER: Someone else.

STUDENT: Shopping.

TEACHER: Tell me more about 'shopping'. What did you think of?

STUDENT: Me shopping for pants.

TEACHER: Were you right there?

STUDENT: You bet.

'Shopping' is written on another section. As the students shared, she extended their words by phrases such as "Tell me more about that", "Was it like a word association?", "Were you right there, in the action?", "Was it a feeling?", "Could you actually see it?" She wrote down exactly what they said, grouping the words, without telling them the pattern she was using.

TEACHER: Can you feel your thinking change and follow another route when you hear the different associations others have made? Interesting, isn't it? Can you tell how I am grouping your ideas as you tell them to me? I am going to give you another word. You will have a chance to try and figure out the patterns. Notice again what happens as you hear the word. This time my word is 'fog'.

Student responses are not evaluated, but are elaborated, extended, built upon.

Make the pattern for the students and allow them to see it inductively.

Practise the thinking in several familiar contexts before introducing the text.

128

She followed the same process, pausing for time to think, then respectfully listening to a variety of students share. She grouped these ideas as well, adding to the words already there.

TEACHER: You are pretty fluent thinkers. Take a moment and talk to the person beside you about what you are noticing about your thinking, and what you think these patterns are.

Students need opportunities to talk and share what's on their minds with their peers.

The room literally buzzed as the students talked about their thinking and the patterns. She allowed three minutes for the conversations, then pulled them together again.

TEACHER: I learned these patterns from a researcher named Bob Marzano. He calls them the 'quadrants of a thought' and suggests that all thoughts are composed of four different ways of thinking— a language component, a visual or image component, an emotional component, and a physical or sensory component. Different words trigger us to start thinking in different quadrants, although some of us almost always start in the same quadrant. It doesn't matter which quadrant you begin in. All are equal. Powerful thinkers move among all the quadrants and use these connections. Sometimes we cannot separate our thinking into discreet quadrants. That, too, is fine. When I am working with a new concept or wish to explore a topic, I can move my thinking around through the quadrants. Marzano calls this 'deep processing'.
  I am going to give you another word. Predict which quadrant you think you will begin in. Write that on your paper. Explain to your partner why you wrote that quadrant.

Extend the experiences into its research base, 'the real world'.

Again she paused and moved among the students. All were intently involved, justifying their patterns of thinking to their partner.

TEACHER: My word is 'lemon'. Resist the urge to share; instead follow your thinking inside your head. [30-40 seconds] Now you can share with your partner. Notice when you are listening if what they say causes you to make different connections and patterns.
  I am going to put on the overhead a poem written by Rita Mendosez called "Lemon". Please read it silently, then on your paper, cluster your thoughts, using the four quadrants as a frame. This is an individual activity.

After the practice, students need individual opportunities to create their own meaning.

The students worked silently for four or five minutes. They looked back and forth from the poem to their papers. The poem was one that could be read in several patterns. As we watched the students, we could see them discover new patterns.

Whole group — individual — partner.

TEACHER: Draw your thinking on this to a temporary close. Did you surprise yourself with where you began? Could you move your response through the four quadrants? Was this easy to do?

Reflection on the process, alone and with others, strengthens and extends individual connections.

Challenging? What did you think of the poem? You have several minutes to talk again to your partner. Notice how your thinking and your responses are similar and different.

Nathalie

LANGUAGE	VISUAL
	HOUSE FILLED WITH LEMONS AND PIE SMELL BICYCLE FUNERAL BAD LEMONADE
PHYSICAL	EMOTIONAL SAD, DISGUSTED, LOVE, HAPPY

ANDY

LANGUAGE	VISUAL
2 DIFFERENT POEMS	COLOUR OF LEMONS
PHYSICAL	EMOTION
THE BITTER TASTE OF LEMONS	WRITTEN AWKWARD HARD TO READ

Again, students talked. The teacher then refocused them by asking who had been surprised by something their partner had said or done in response to the poem. Many of the students commented on the various ways to read the poem and which way they had first started. The variety of responses ranged from comments on the poet's relationship with her husband to the bitter taste of the lemon to reactions to the physical structure of the poem.

GLENDA: I found this easy because things just popped into my head and I wrote them down.

ANDY: I found that it was easy when everyone had shared their opinions.

TEACHER: I am going to change my second way of looking at a poem. This time I am using a poem "Apparitions" by Edwin Varney. I will put it on the overhead, read it to you twice, and ask you to think about it. Notice where your mind takes you.

This poem was quite different from the previous poem. The teacher read it through twice, not pausing for comments or for sharing.

TEACHER: On your paper please write down three words that you could use to represent your thinking about this poem. Now, turn to your partner and compare your three words. I will give you several minutes to see if you can come to consensus on three words that would represent your combined thinking about the poem.

Students talked in pairs, then returned to the whole-class group. The teacher modeled how to make a Concept Map using this number of words. Three words were randomly chosen from the class and written

This second time does not direct collecting personal reactions or prior experience, but allows students to connect as they read the poem.

Collecting three words to represent their thinking invites students to synthesize what is really important to them in the poem.

The negotiation extends and deepens understanding.

Attaching explicit language to connect the words reorganizes the student's thinking.

130

on the board. She drew lines to connect them, and asked the students to explain to her the connections among the words that showed an understanding of the poem. She wrote the connections on the lines.

TEACHER: We are returning to an individual activity. Take the three words that you agreed upon, and make a *Concept Map* that illustrates your understanding of the poem.

Once you have completed that, please free write for several minutes to tell me what the poem means to you.

NATHALIE:

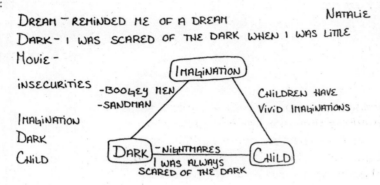

I see the dark as something that sort of rolls or creeps in slowly.
It makes me think of being helpless, like something is chasing me.

GLENDA:

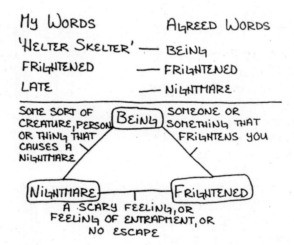

This poem reminds me of myself after I read the book *Helter Skelter*. Every little noise or movement scared me. The end of the poem really grabs me because at the end of my dream I was always being chased by Charles Manson and it was too late to escape.

As observers, we were very impressed with the concentration of the students, and their evident ease with handling the pace of the lesson.

TEACHER: This is the third and final response form that I want you to try. Have you been thinking about which of the first two is the most comfortable for you?

This poem is called, ''what ugly is'' by Robert Priest. Before you read the poem, please write individually what comes to your mind in response to that title. This is an individual write.

Vary the format by inviting personal connections prior to reading.

This free write lasted three minutes, then the teacher placed the poem on the overhead and read it to them. This time, they had moved directly from an individual activity to a whole-group activity.

JULIE: *Pre-write:* I think of my cousin and where she lives. I think of sludge and the Teenage Mutant Ninja Turtle and where they live. I think of people with burns, I feel sorry for them. I wonder about the poem I'm about to read. I think of myself in the morning or anyone in the morning, garbage dumps, messy rooms, wrinkles, fat.

TEACHER: Another way of responding is to think of the connections that we make. Some people think of connections in terms of four categories:

The format encourages connections among self and various communities in the world, in and out of the classroom.

Individual — Whole Group.

- self;
- literary, i.e., what have we read and what we have seen;
- societal, i.e., the community of those around us, in the class, in the school, in our communities;
- historical, i.e., patterns that have been repeated in history or in the world at large.

Using these categories as your frame, write to show an understanding of the poem.

JULIE: After reading the poem: I did most of those connections. I also think about the feelings evoked by unloved people, how sorry and how ugly that thought is. Literary is the movie *The Fisher King*. Social is not enough for everyone. Hurting is ugly.

After a five-minute write, the students shared with one another. The teacher invited them to question any vocabulary or phrase in the poem that caused them confusion or caused them to wonder. They moved easily from conversation to conversation.

Whole-group clarification and questions occur after small group and individual searches for meaning.

TEACHER: This is your final response for me. Remember that I asked you to think on several channels. I am interested in what you noticed about your thinking. Which of these frames made it easiest for you to read and respond to the poems? Did anything about your thinking surprise you? Which do you think you could most easily use again? What advice would you give me if I use this lesson design in the future?

JULIE: I just didn't know how to categorize myself. Now, I do. I know that I am an emotions first thinker.

NATHALIE: I am visual. I like just letting my thoughts flow on paper. I keep my mind open and thoughts flow.

ANDY: I'm gonna spend the rest of the day thinking about my brain.

KRIS: A longer session (I know it can't be helped, but. . .)

Reflection guides students toward increasing amounts of independence in response.

The Next Class

After exposure to several more poems, connecting and relating them through the frames to the students' experiences and the world of the poet's experiences, students were given several poems from which to choose. They wrote in response to the poem, using one of the three frames as their 'connector', responding in a way that showed they understood the poem.

QUADRANTS OF A THOUGHT

1. Choose several words to use as prompts and encourage the students to notice what first comes into their minds when the prompt is given, and then where their thinking travels next.

2. Build the categories for the *Quadrants of a Thought* with the students.

language	images
physical sensations	emotions

3. Have students predict if there is a pattern to the quadrant that generally sparks their thinking.

4. Use the title of a poem or a topic to begin to connect the *Quadrants of a Thought* to the text/experience.

5. Present the text and have the students jot notes or cluster their responses to the poem, using the frame of the quadrants.

6. Students compare their thinking and their responses with a partner.

COLLABORATIVE CONCEPT MAP

1. Read a poem twice to the students.

2. Each student chooses three words that represent his or her thinking about this poem.

3. With a partner, students negotiate for three words that they agree could represent the poem to them. (This step can be repeated in groups of 4.)

4. Construct a *Concept Map* with the three words. The connecting lines hold the language that explains the connections among the words and with the poem.

5. Each student constructs a *Concept Map* with their shared key words.

6. Each student writes to explain his or her understanding of the poem.

CONNECTIONS

1. Students free write on the poem's title.

2. Read the poem as a group.

3. Explain the connecting categories as those of connections to self, literary associations, societal associations, historical associations.

4. Students write to show an understanding of the poem, using these connecting frames.

FRAME

1. Students explore three response frameworks.

2. Students continually reflect, alone and with others, about their response to each of the frameworks.

3. Students notice changes in the patterns of their thinking through the use of different frameworks and opportunities to talk.

4. Students write an extended response to one of the three poems.

14

Daedalus and Icarus . . .
A Learning Sequence

For most of us as teachers, the unit of instruction is not the lesson; the lesson is just a piece of something larger. The better we get as teachers, the more we think about how our lessons hang together.

— L. Shulman, *On Research on Teaching: A Conversation with Lee Shulman*

Literacy's most profound function is to help connect the individual with larger and larger circles of reference, which ultimately come to constitute the meaning of his or her life.

— R. Brown, *Schools of Thought*

One of the keys to effectively digesting and learning from experience is to deliberately set out to represent such learning in different ways and from different points of view. Elaboration is most successful when it engages all body/mind systems . . . generating associations with more of what we already know.

— R.N. Caine & G. Caine, *Making Connections*

Achievement in nearly every area of human endeavour would probably be enhanced if the relevant concepts and how they function were understood and used to interpret events . . . concept maps not only help students to gain meaningful knowledge . . . they also enhance positive feeling and acting during and after the experience . . .

— J.D. Novak & D.B. Gowin, *Learning How To Learn*

The grade eight humanities students have been studying versions of the Icarus story through art and literature. The class is about to reflect on the strategy sequence they've used to study the Penelope Farmer version, Daedalus and Icarus. Their files are open. They are reviewing their samples before they begin a Concept Map. On the chalkboard is their strategy outline.

Connecting	Processing	Personalizing/ Transforming
Think-of-a-Time • when someone gave you advice and you didn't listen	**Matching Thinking** • eight parts	**Concept Mapping**
Building from Clues • using four quadrants • track thinking in clusters	**Listen-Sketch-Draft**	• phrases from the text

TEACHER: Let's return to our sequence and focus on key ideas. Today you will determine the most important ideas in the story and link them in a *Concept Map*.

In the *Think-of-a-Time* strategy you examined a time when someone offered you advice and you didn't listen. Then you thought of a time when you witnessed someone not listening to advice, and finally you recalled a time when you helped someone who hadn't listened to advice. Let's hear someone's three stories.

The students referred to their Think-of-a-Time response sheets.

JONI: I went to an amusement park in Washington, D.C. I had never been on a giant roller coaster before. My cousins had and I wanted to show them I wasn't scared so I decided to go on. My Mom told me not to, but I did. I got to the front of the line and fainted.   *Personal experience*

JONI: When I was watching kids playing around the pool, their Mom kept saying "Don't run" and they kept running. Sure enough, the little boy fell and skinned his knee and howled!   *Witnessing*

JONI: One of my friends went and shoplifted and I told him not to. He did and got arrested. His Mom and Dad paid a fine and he was grounded for two months.   *Helper*

TEACHER: Thank you. In your groups, pull some common elements from your stories of not heeding advice.

Students, in groups of four, quickly began talking. They reviewed their stories and collected common elements that threaded them. These were listed on the board:

Link personal experience to that of others.

- stubborn behavior
- a crisis usually happens
- people feel sorry
- sometimes the advice is wrong
- consequences
- pain

TEACHER: In your second sample using the *Building from Clues* strategy, you talked about phrases from the story using the *Four Quadrants of a Thought* as an organizer.

The teacher revealed the phrases on the overhead and then drew the four quadrants on the chalkboard.

- marvellous intentions
- cast into the prison
- feathers also from birds
- exploring all the while
- stare at them
- seized by still greater joy
- failed to watch
- forgotten all warnings

language	images
physical sensation	emotions

TEACHER: I read a phrase, you talked to your partner, and then we shared connections. You tracked your thinking after working with three clues.

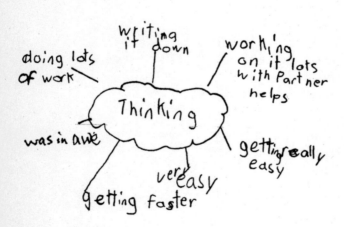

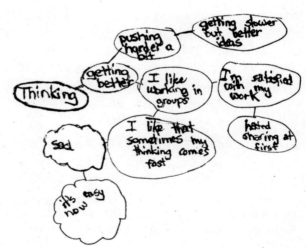

138

TEACHER: You created collaborative drafts.

Marvellous inventions
Cast into the prison
Feathers also from birds
Explaining all the while
Stare at them
Seized by still greater joy
Failed to watch
Forgotten all warnings

ORCO THE MAGNIFICENT

Orco, the magnificent inventor got a job working for the king. He invented tons of things: electric shoe polisher, invisible hairbrush, no-wash shirt, disposible underwear. These marvellous inventions were admired by everyone in the kingdom.

Orco's most recent inventions was the wings. A pair of Dodo birds wings 65" x 45" wings span to be exact. For these wings he used fathers perfume. Feathers also from birds were used.

Orco spent the 375 days perfecting his invention. He was warned that the invention would not

work. Forgotten all warning he climbed to a high point on the "Ridge" and he jumped! The people failed to watch.

Orco swiftly glided across the sky. He landed before the village people. He turned around just to stare at them because he thought they looked funny. Anyhow, the people were seized by joy that Orco was alive. They were seized by still greater joy when they realized the wings worked. Everyone was happy.

They threw a party in Orco's honour. Orco was explaining all the while how his invention was made.

The king was upset about all the publicity. This silly stunt would bring his royal kingdom. So he convinced everyone Orco was crazy and Orco was casted into prison.

The End

TEACHER: You used the criteria that we had developed for powerful stories to assess your drafts. You wrote *Dear Me* notes offering yourself advice. Let's hear someone's advice.

KELLY: Dear Me:
    I think you have been thinking very hard and I am proud of you. Maybe you could add a little more action and senses to make it more interesting.

TEACHER: For homework you composed your own version. When you returned, we listened to a number of drafts and refined the criteria before you presented your draft to your group. We studied the story two ways. First we used *Matching Thinking*. Do you remember the new way we used groups?

SHIRI: You gave one part of the story to each group. I think we had eight groups.

Nodding heads confirmed the number.

CHANDRA: We read our part and created a summary. We prepared a way to present it to the class.

WAYNE: I think that's when we tried to figure out which part started the story. As a class, we worked really hard deciding the order. When we decided, we got to hear the group read it again in a great way. Remember Jason's group's sound effects?

Nods confirmed recall.

TEACHER: You heard the author's version when we used the *Listen-Sketch-Draft* Strategy. In your groups, look back through the four segments you sketched and wrote about. Talk to one another about important ideas.

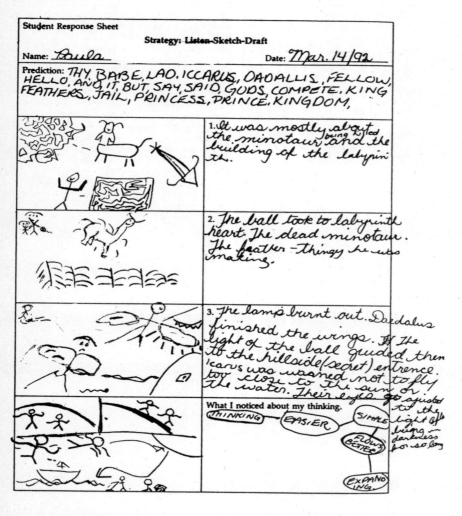

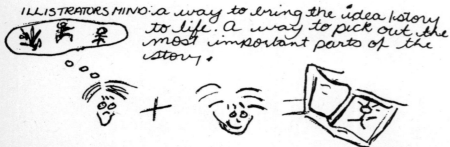

*The talk flowed in each small group. The students reflected
sophisticated understandings of a complex text. After a few minutes,
the teacher signalled the familiar five seconds.*

TEACHER: You seem to have developed deep connections with this
myth. Now I am going to show you how to build a *Concept Map*.
First we'll create one together, then you and your partner will
create one on your own.

We need to determine the most important ideas from this version
of *Daedalus and Icarus*. With your partner, brainstorm a list of key
ideas down the side of your page.

*A student distributed large sheets of newsprint, one to each set of
partners. As the partners received their paper, they began negotiating
their "big idea" lists. The teacher drew six circles randomly on the
board as the students negotiated shared lists.*

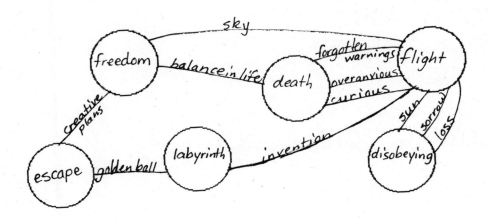

TEACHER: Look at your list of ideas. I need six key ideas to begin
our mapping. Who has one to offer?

*All suggestions were accepted until there were six words placed in
the blank circles.*

TEACHER: Let's consider that these six words hold the essence of
the myth. Think of ways to connect these words that will show
you understand the myth.

*The students pondered and pointed to words, indicating that they
were beginning to find ways to link the ideas.*

TEACHER: Can you see ways to connect these words?

ARRON: Connect *flight* and *freedom* with sky.

TEACHER: How are you connecting them?

ARRON: The sky felt like freedom for Icarus. The thrill of the
           flight was his path to freedom.

TEACHER: Thank you . . . Another connection?

CHRISTIAN: Connect *labyrinth* and *escape* with *golden ball* because it was the trail for escape.

The teacher pressed each participant to support the connections. She pulled from each contribution key words to write on the linking line.

ROBBIE: Connect *flight* and *disobeying* with *too close to sun*. Icarus forgot or maybe he didn't believe his Dad's warnings. You know how parents sometimes exaggerate a little. He was having a great time riding in the air.

Each connection was elaborated through talk. The teacher invited other class members to offer insights related to the way the volunteers were connecting, adding new dimensions.

TEACHER: What do you notice about these connections?

SULLIVAN: You really need to take time to think about each one.

JONI: It's tricky to choose only a few words.

TEACHER: You are right. Synthesizing our ideas can be challenging! Now, work with your partner to create your own map. You don't have to have any set number of circles. Use this time to really push your thinking.

The class settled into quiet deliberations. The teacher listened in on the conversations, helping individuals to reach for meaningful evidence. After about twenty minutes, she invited partners to discuss their powerful connections. The students delighted in sharing the nuances of their connections. Volunteers added further details. The challenge of this assessment set a buzz of excitement in the room.

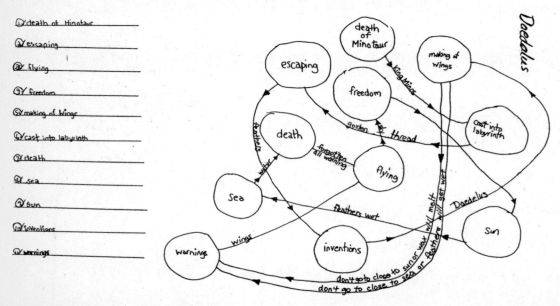

TEACHER: Before you leave, let's choose criteria to aim for in your personal *Concept Maps*.

- few, well-chosen words;
- connections from all four quadrants;
- 6-8 circles;
- specific story vocabulary.

For homework, create your own map of this Daedalus and Icarus Story. Using this criteria, rate yours on a scale: Powerful, Competent, Developing, or Undeveloped and give reasons why. Thank you for your hard work today. I certainly learned a lot from your connections.

Students smiled. They found it rewarding that she really did learn from them.

The Next Class

The students moved into different small groups to present and give feedback on their homework assignments. Several examples were shared with the whole class. Students then reflected in their logs, offering advice to themselves for the next time they created maps.

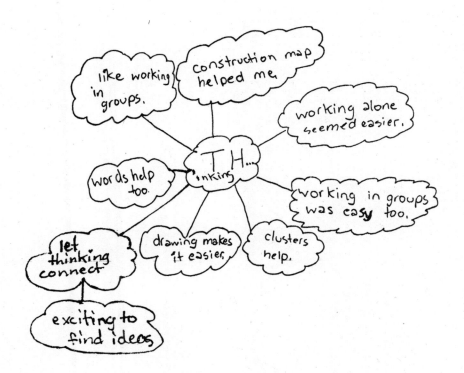

I felt a part of me was dying
when Icarus fell from the sky.
It was all my fault. Icarus was
far too young and immature
to handle the responsibility.
Although I have to admit
the feeling is great... To soar
above the trees, boats, the
labyrinth, the king — to laugh
in his face. I felt free and
uncontrolable. Poor boy, the feeling
was just too strong for him to
handle. I've accepted this and
must be with the loss forever.

J.J.

Later, in writer's workshop, some students chose to use their
Concept Maps as a springboard for writing.

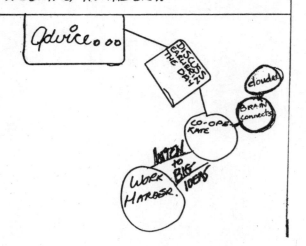

Part 4 ICARUS LISTENED BUT DIDN'T HEAR. THEY STARTED
TO FLAP THEIR ARMS... THEY DIDN'T SUCEED AT
FIRST. AFTER A WHILE THEY SOARED IN THE AIR.
PEOPLE WATCHED THEM, THOUGHT THEY WERE
GODS. ICARUS GOT TO CLOSE TO THE WATER. THEN HE
GOT TOO CLOSE TO THE SUN. FEATHERS DROPPED TILL
THERE WAS NOT ENOUGH LEFT TO HOLD FEED HIM.
HE FELL TO THE SEE AND DAEDELEUS WAS
LEFT WEEPING IN THE SKY.

FOUR QUADRANTS

1. Students work with a partner.

2. Students view an illustration or artifact; read or listen to a passage using the *Four Quadrants of a Thought* as an organizer.

3. Students sometimes gather data from each interaction in idea sketches, clusters, or lists.

4. Students share their understandings with a partner and then with the whole class.

5. Four to six pictures, artifacts, or passages are processed.

6. Students reflect on what they noticed about their thinking or learning using the strategy.

7. Students use the information to generate predictions, draw conclusions, determine key ideas, generate questions, or offer hypotheses.

VARIATIONS

a) Students are grouped in partners with one partner facing the screen and the other with his or her back to the screen.

b) A visual—object, picture, graph, or passage—is revealed. Partner A, facing the screen, describes the item using the four quadrants as an organizer. Partner B jots down ideas and asks questions. Partners change roles.

c) Sometimes the partners are in groups of four, with two A's facing the screen, and two B's listening and gathering data. The advantage here is that the two A's or B's can negotiate meaning.

CONCEPT MAPPING

1. In partners, students generate a list of key ideas from the focus of study.

2. The teacher draws a number of circles on the chalkboard, chart paper, or overhead projector.

3. Students offer key ideas to be placed in the circles.

4. Students think of *evidence* to link two keys. The teacher presses for words, phrases, illustrations that reflect deep meaning, often using the four quadrants as an organizer.

5. Students continue connecting ideas. The teacher invites the whole class to offer advice when one person is searching for words to show understanding. Key ideas can be connected any number of ways.

6. Partners collaboratively generate a map. Connections are shared as the class of learners is engaged in the process.

7. The teacher invites the learners to identify attributes of powerful connection.

8. Partners orally, and eventually in writing, assess their maps using the criteria.

9. Students generate their own maps.

10. Students reflect on how the map shows understanding.

TO ASSESS CONCEPT MAPS

In reflection with the students, continually model that quality, not quantity, is the key to a *Concept Map*.

1. Develop criteria for powerful connections with the students.

2. Invite the students to assess their collaborative or individual maps using the criteria.

3. Invite students to offer themselves advice for the next time they map their learning.

4. Some teachers award points: one point for each key idea and one point for each linking word.

MATCHING THINKING

1. An article or story is divided into parts.

2. Students are divided into the same number of groups. Parts are distributed, one per group.

3. Each group's initial task is to read the passage and generate a story that would include their part of the text. They prepare to read their part in an original way.

4. As a whole class, they negotiate the order of the parts—forming hypotheses and offering support from text clues.

5. Students reflect on how the process helped them construct their own understandings, and on how they might approach the task next time.

6. The story is studied in partners as independent reading or using a strategy, then the author's order is compared to the order of the class.

VARIATIONS

a) Pictures or artifacts can be used to generate hypotheses or questions.

b) Small groups of students can be given a scrambled text. They work together to justify the construction of the passage. They present their version to another small group. The teacher has the text on overhead acetate pieces. As the pieces are discussed, they are ordered. In this case, two overhead projectors work well.

15

Learners Reflect

Change happens in classrooms when teachers listen intently to their students and teach responsively. In Mary Daniels' ceramics class, she asks students to self-evaluate at the end of term. She includes a list of specific techniques that have been taught. Students rank themselves as having shown some improvement or great improvement. Following this, she asks four questions:

1. How do you feel about your progress this term?
2. What should I notice when I assess your studio component of the program?
3. What has been the most important aspect of this course for you?
4. What can I change to make this course help you become a better artist?

What is valued is explicit. The dialogue between student and teacher respects the learner, keeps the focus on personal change toward individual and group goals, and informs the teacher. It is ongoing and informative to all participants.

Our goal is to always empower our learners, to make them increasingly independent, and to be able to think and learn in increasingly diverse and flexible ways. We present the menu of our strategies to learners, support their development in thinking with these strategies, then step aside and allow the personalization to happen. Karalee, our typist, reflects on her strategic use.

Effective study skills would have been the most useful tools that I could have developed in secondary school. If I had developed the techniques that I did last year at university when I was in high school, I would have had a tremendous advantage. After exposure to a wide variety of strategies and a fair amount of experimentation, I have developed some techniques for studying that are very efficient and produce incredible results *every* time.

My favorite technique, the one I use for essays and exams, is the *Concept Map*. It took me a while to pick it up because I couldn't see how a map with bubbles and lines could help me with a university-level course. I often decided that it was too close to the exam to start playing around with drawings. I ran a mini-experiment

on myself and four similar exams in my 200 level
Psychology course. For my first exam, I used my old
way of studying—highlighting, notes, etc.—and
received a B−. Then I practiced with notes and *Concept
Maps* on the next two exams and got an A. I took a
risk and used only *Concept Maps* for my final. It took
half the time to study. When I wrote the exam, I knew
the answer to every question and the material came to
me with ease. The ''A+'' that I received definitely
convinced me. And I still remember what I studied.

Maureen McDermid organized a Forum on Enrichment in
Secondary Education. Students who were currently attending
university reflected on what had been effective in their secondary
years. Their comments ranged from time management, critical
thinking skills, the ability to explore information and question
themselves through a family feeling and group projects that helped
them learn about group interaction. In a group write to synthesize
their ideas for the teachers, the students wrote,

A teacher of the '90s should also be able to realize
when learning is actually taking place. With this,
we mean that they should be able to realize when
the student has grasped the concept at hand, and
then set him or her on his or her way. The teacher
of the '90s should be a leader, not a dictator.

We have honed our practice to be able to put many of these
enabling conditions in place for all students. It is time to put aside
the chalk and interact with our students and our content in
meaningful ways.

Bibliography

Reference Books

Archbald, D.A. & F.M. Newmann. *Beyond Standardized Testing: Assessing Authentic Academic Achievement in the Secondary School.* Reston, VA: National Association of Secondary School Principals, 1988.

Armstrong, T. *Awakening Your Child's Natural Genius.* Los Angeles, CA: J.P. Tarcher, Inc.

Atwell, N. *Side by Side: Essays on Teaching to Learn.* Portsmouth, NH: Heinemann Educational Books, Inc., 1991.

Bellanca, J. & R. Fogarty. *Blueprints for Thinking in the Cooperative Classroom.* Palatine, IL: Skylight Publishing, 1990.

Brandt, R. "On Research on Teaching: A Conversation with Lee Shulman." *Educational Leadership.* 49(7), 14-19, 1992.

Brown, R.G. *Schools of Thought.* San Francisco, CA: Jossey-Bass Inc., 1991.

Brownlie, F. "The Art of Strategic Connections." In A. Costa, J. Bellanca & R. Fogarty (Eds.), *If Minds Matter: A Foreword to the Future, Vol. II.* Palatine, IL: Skylight Publishing, 1992.

Brownlie, C.F., S. Close & L. Wingren. *Reaching for Higher Thought.* Edmonton, AB: Arnold Publishing, 1988.

Brownlie, C.F., S. Close & L. Wingren. *Tomorrow's Classroom Today.* Markham, ON: Pembroke Publishing, 1990.

Bull, G. & M. Anstey. "Achieving Independent Learning: Drawing Genre and Process Together." In Fiona McKay (Ed.), *Public and Private Lessons, The Language of Teaching and Learning.* Carlton, Victoria: Australian Reading Association, 1991.

Caine, R.N. & G. Caine. *Teaching and the Human Brain.* Alexandria, VA: Association for Supervision and Curriculum Development, 1991.

Centennial Case Study Project Group. *Cases for Teaching in the Secondary School.* Coquitlam, B.C.: Centennial Secondary School, 1991.

Close, S. "Is What We Are Doing Giving Us What We Want?" *Making Connections.* 2(4), 4-12, 1992.

Corey, S.R. *Principle-Centered Leadership.* New York: Summit Books, 1991.

D'Arcy, P. *Making Sense, Shaping Meaning.* Portsmouth, NH: Heinemann Educational Books Inc., 1989.

Duckworth, E. "Twenty-Four, Twenty-Two, and I Love You: Keeping It Complex." *Harvard Educational Review,* 61(1), 1-23, 1991.

Duffelmeyer, F.A. & D.D. Baum. "The Extended Anticipation Guide." *Journal of Reading,* 35(8), 654-656, 1992.

Elbow, P. *Writing Without Teachers.* New York: Oxford University Press, 1982.

Eisner, E.W. *The Enlightened Eye.* New York: Macmillan, 1991.

Eisner, E.W. "Taking a Second Look: Educational Connoisseurship Revisited." In M.W. McLaughlin & D.C. Phillips (Eds.), *Evaluation and Education: At Quarter Century — Ninetieth Yearbook of the National Society for the Study of Education, Part II.* Chicago, IL: University of Chicago Press, 1991.

Evertson, C.M. & R. Weade. "The Social Construction of Classroom Lessons." In H.C. Waxman & H.J. Walberg (Eds.), *Effective Teaching: Current Research.* Chicago, IL: The National Society for the Study of Education, 1991.

Fisher, D. "Portfolio Assessment: A Framework for a Range of Options." *Research Forum.* 9, 9-12, 1992.

Forrestal, P. "Response: Group Work and Oracy." In G. Boomer, *Fair Dinkum Teaching and Learning.* Upper Montclair, NJ: Boynton/Cook Publishers, 1985.

Fulghum, R. *It Was on Fire When I Lay Down on It.* New York: Ballantine Books, 1988.

Fullan, M.G. *The New Meaning of Educational Change.* New York: Teachers College Press, 1991.

Gardner, H. *The Unschooled Mind.* New York: Basic Books, 1991.

Gardner, H. Foreward. In D. Lazear, *Seven Ways of Knowing.* Palatine, IL: Skylight Publishing, 1991.

Gardner, H. *The Mind's New Science.* New York: Basic Books, 1987.

Goleman, D., P. Kaufman & M. Ray. "The Art of Creativity." *Psychology Today.* 25(2), 40-47, 1992.

Gregory, K. & C. Cameron. "Anecdotal Reporting: One District's Search for a Reporting Process that Enhances Learning." *Research Forum.* 9, 13-16, 1992.

Gross, R. *Peak Learning.* Los Angeles, CA: J.P. Tarcher, Inc., 1991.

Healy, J.M. *Endangered Minds.* New York: Simon and Schuster, 1991.

Hill, S. & T. Hill. *The Collaborative Classroom.* Portsmouth, NH: Heinemann Educational Books Inc., 1990.

Hull, G., M. Rose, C. Greenleaf & B. Reilly. "Seeing the Promise of the Underprepared." *The Quarterly.* 13(1), 6-13, 1991.

Hurd, P.D. "Why We Must Transform Science Education." *Educational Leadership.* 49(2), 33-35, 1991.

Jeroski, S. "Learner-focused Assessment: Helping Students Grow." *Research Forum.* 9, 27-33, 1992.

Jeroski, S., F. Brownlie & L. Kaser. *Reading and Responding: Evaluation Resources for Teachers, Gr. 6.* Scarborough, ON: Nelson Canada, 1991.

Johnson, D.W. & R.T. Johnson. "Classroom Instruction and Cooperative Learning." In H.C. Waxman & H.J. Walberg (Eds.), *Effective Teaching: Current Research.* Chicago, IL: The National Society for the Study of Education, 1991.

Katz, L.G. & S.C. Chard. *Engaging Children's Minds: The Project Approach.* Norwood, NJ: Ablex Publishing Co., 1991.

Kirschenbaum, R.J. "An Interview with Howard Gardner." *Gifted Child Today*, Nov./Dec., 26-32, 1990.

Knight, S.L. & H.C. Waxman. "Students' Cognition and Classroom Instruction." In H.C. Waxman & H.J. Walberg (Eds.), *Effective Teaching: Current Research*. Chicago, IL: The National Society for the Study of Education, 1991.

Lazear, D. *Seven Ways of Knowing*. Palatine, IL: Skylight Publishing, 1991.

Lazear, D. "Seven Ways of Knowing." In A. Costa, J. Bellanca & R. Fogarty (Eds.), *If Minds Matter: A Foreword to the Future, Vol. II*. Palatine, IL: Skylight Publishing, 1992.

McFadden, J., C. Flynn & B. Bazzo. *Lifescience: Making Your Life a Success*. Sydney, Australia: Horwitz Grahame Books Pty. Ltd., 1986.

McLaren, M. "The Search for Understanding." *The Best of Teaching*. (Fall). Vancouver, B.C.: Provincial Intermediate Teachers' Association, 1990.

McNally, D. *Even Eagles Need a Push*. New York: Bantam Doubleday Dell Publishing Group, Inc., 1990.

Marzano, R.J. & D.E. Arrendondo. *Tactics for Thinking*. Aurora, CO: Mid-Continent Regional Educational Laboratory, 1986.

Marzano, R.J., R.S. Brandt, C.S. Hughes, B.F. Jones, B.Z. Presseisen, S.C. Rankin & C. Suhor. *Dimensions of Thinking: A Framework for Curriculum and Instruction*. Alexandria, VA: Association for Supervision and Curriculum Development, 1988.

Ministry of Education and Ministry Responsible for Multiculturalism and Human Rights. *The Intermediate Program: Foundations, Draft*. Victoria, B.C.: Ministry of Education and Ministry Responsible for Multiculturalism and Human Rights, 1992.

Ministry of Education and Ministry Responsible for Multiculturalism and Human Rights. *Thinking in the Classroom, Vol. 1 & 2*. Victoria, B.C.: Assessment, Examinations & Reporting Branch, 1991.

Minstrell, J.A., "Teaching Sciences for Understanding." In L.B. Resnick & L.E. Klopfer (Eds.), *Toward the Thinking Curriculum: Current Cognitive Research*. Alexandria, VA: Association for Supervision and Curriculum Development, 1989.

Newmann, F.M. "Linking Restructuring to Authentic Student Achievement." *Phi Delta Kappan*. 72(6), 458-463, 1991.

Newmann, F.M. "Making Small Groups Productive." *Issues in Restructuring Schools*, 2, 1-3, 1992.

Novak, J.D. & D.B. Gowin. *Learning How to Learn*. Cambridge, England: Cambridge University Press, 1984.

Nystrand, M. & A. Gamoran. "Student Engagement: When Recitation Becomes Conversation." In H.C. Waxman & H.J. Walberg (Eds.), *Effective Teaching: Current Research*. Chicago, IL: The National Society for the Study of Education, 1991.

Parker, W.C. *Renewing the Social Studies Curriculum*. Alexandria, VA: Association for Supervision and Curriculum Development, 1991.

Pearson, D.P., L.R. Roehler, J.A. Dole & G.G. Duffy. *Developing Expertise in Reading Comprehension: What Should Be Taught?* Champaign, IL: University of Illinois Centre for the Study of Reading, Technical Report, No. 512, 1990.

Perkins, D.N. "Educating for Insight." *Educational Leadership*. 49(2), 4-8, 1991.

Probst, R.E. "Literature as exploration and the classroom." In E.J. Farrell & J.R. Squire (Eds.), *Transactions with literature: A fifty year perspective*. Urbana, IL: National Council of Teachers of English, 1990.

Reid, J., P. Forrestal & J. Cook. *Small Group Learning in the Classroom*. Rozelle, NSW: Chalkface Press, 1989.

Rico, G.L. *Pain and Possibility*. Los Angeles, CA: J.P. Tarcher, 1991.

Rico, G.L. "Daedalus and Icarus Within: The Literature/Art/Writing Connection." *English Journal*. 78 (3), 14-23, 1989.

Rico, G.L., *Writing the Natural Way*. Los Angeles, CA: J.P. Tarcher, 1983.

Rief, L., *Seeking Diversity*. Portsmouth, NH: Heinemann Educational Books Inc., 1992.

Rieneke, Z. & H. Gardner. "Authentic Assessment: Beyond the Buzzword and Into the Classroom." In V. Perrone (Ed.), *Expanding Student Assessment*. Alexandria, VA: Association for Supervision and Curriculum Development, 1991.

Rosen, H. (1992). "Why is the narrative story so important to children in their journey to become literate?" In O. Cochrane, (Ed.), *Questions & Answers About Whole Language*. Katoneh, NY: Richard C. Owen Publishers.

Sanders, D.A. & J.A. Sanders. *Teaching Creativity Through Metaphor*. New York: Longman Inc., 1984.

Schlechty, P.C. *Schools for the 21st Century: Leadership Imperatives for Educational Reform*. San Francisco, CA: Jossey-Bass, Inc., 1990.

Scriven, M. "Beyond Formative and Summative Evaluation." In M.W. McLaughlin & D.C. Phillips (Eds.), *Evaluation and Education: At Quarter Century — Ninetieth Yearbook of the National Society for the Study of Education, Part II*. Chicago, IL: University of Chicago Press, 1991.

Senge, P.M. *The Fifth Discipline: The Art and Practice of the Learning Organization*. New York: Doubleday, 1990.

Sinetar, M. *Developing a 21st Century Mind*. New York: Villard Books, 1991.

Smith, F. *to think*. New York: Teachers College Press, 1990.

Smith, K. "Explain content area inquiry and how it affects intermediate students." In O. Cochrane, (Ed.), *Questions & Answers About Whole Language*. Katoneh, NY: Richard C. Owen Publishers, 1992.

Smith, K. "Entertaining a Text: A Reciprocal Process." In K.G. Short & K.M. Pierce (Eds.), *Talking About Books*. Portsmouth, NH: Heinemann Educational Books Inc., 1990.

Stiggins, R.J. "Assessment Literacy." *Phi Delta Kappan*. 72 (7), 534-539, 1991.

Tierney, R.J. "Ongoing Research and New Directions." In J.W. Irwin & M.A. Doyle (Eds.), *Reading/Writing Connections: Learning from Research*. Newark, NJ: International Reading Association, 1992.

Tierney, R.J., M.A. Carter & L.E. Desai. *Portfolio Assessment in the Reading-Writing Classroom.* Norwood, MA: Christopher Gordon Publishers, Inc., 1991.

Tobin, K. & B.J. Fraser. "Learning from Exemplary Teachers." In H.C. Waxman & H.J. Walberg (Eds.), *Effective Teaching: Current Research.* Berkeley, CA: The National Society for the Study of Education, 1991.

Tyler, R.W. "General Statement on Program Evaluation." In M.W. McLaughlin & D.C. Phillips (Eds.), *Evaluation and Education: At Quarter Century—Nineteenth Yearbook of the National Society for the Study of Education, Part II.* Chicago, IL: University of Chicago Press, 1991.

vasSavant, M. *Brain Building.* New York: Bantam Books, 1990.

Walsh, D. "Presentation on Behalf of American Federation of Teachers." Sonoma, CA: Sonoma State College, 1986.

White, N., T. Blythe & H. Gardner. "Multiple Intelligences Theory: Creating the Thoughtful Classroom." In A. Costa, J. Bellanca & R. Fogarty (Eds.), *If Minds Matter: A Foreword to the Future, Vol. II.* Palatine, IL: Skylight Publishing, 1992.

Wilkinson, A. & L. Stratta. "Listening and the Teaching of English." As quoted in G. Boomer, *Fair Dinkum Teaching and Learning.* Upper Montclair, NJ: Boynton/Cook Publishers, 1977.

Wlodkowski, R.J. & J.H. Jayne. *Eager to Learn.* San Francisco, CA: Jossey-Bass Publishers, 1990.

Wonder, J. & P. Donovan. *The Flexibility Factor.* New York: Ballantine Books, 1989.

Student Books

Alper, L. Project Director. Patterns in Mathematics, *Interactive Mathematics Project.* Berkley, CA: EQUAL, Lawrence Hall of Science, University of California, 1992.

Cherry, L. *A River Ran Wild.* Orlando, FL: Harcourt, Brace, Jovanovich, 1992.

Eliot, T.S. "The Love Song of J. Alfred Prufrock." In M.L. Iveson, J.E. Oster & J.K. McClay (Ed.), *Literary Experiences, Volume 2.* Scarborough, ON: Prentice-Hall Canada Inc., 1990.

Farmer, P. "Daedalus and Icarus." In John McInnes (Sr. Author), *Mirror Images.* Scarborough, ON: Nelson Canada, 1989.

Garnier, K. *Our Elders Speak.* White Rock, B.C.: Karie Garnier, 1990.

Johnson, P. "The Two Sisters." In C. Gerson, (Ed.), *Vancouver Short Stories.* Vancouver, B.C.: University of British Columbia Press, 1985.

Kuang N. "A Ge-Ware Incense Burner." In Sharon Jeroski (Ed.), *Tapestries.* Scarborough, On: Nelson-Canada, 1991.

Scieszka, Jon. *The True Story of the Three Little Pigs! by A. Wolf.* New York: Viking Kestrel, 1989.

Sleator, W. *Singularity.* New York: E.P. Dutton, 1985.

Veighey, C. "Operation Survival." In R.J. Scott (Ed.), *Sense and Feeling.* Toronto: Copp Clark Pitman, 1982.

Effort	Plan

ANTICIPATION GUIDE

Name

Block

Date

Answer Yes or No. Support your response.

	You	Writer

Reflection:

Developing Intelligences

1	2	3	4	5
undeveloped			highly developed	

Seven Intelligences	What I know about myself	What I noticed today	Advice for next time
Verbal/Linguistic			
Logical/Mathematical			
Visual/Spatial			
Musical/Rhythmic			
Body/Kinesthetic			
Interpersonal			
Intrapersonal			

Reponse Sheet

Strategy: Responding with Key Ideas

Name(s): _____

Date(s): _____

What I know about experts

Big Ideas	Big Ideas
Big Ideas	Self-assessment about my big ideas
Questions	Questions
about my learning	advice for next time

Think-of-a-Time

Name(s): _____ Date(s): _____

Student Reponse Sheet

Strategy: Listen-Sketch-Draft

Name: _____ Date: _____

Prediction	
1.	2.
3.	4.
5.	6.

What I noticed about my thinking.